CHILDREN OF THE EAST

Also by Leonard Davis

Residential Care: A Community Resource
Janus Publishing Company, London, 1993
(First edition, Heinemann, 1982)

Sex and the Social Worker
Janus Publishing Company, London, 1993
(First edition, Heinemann, 1983)

Pastoral Care: Caring for Secondary School Pupils
Janus Publishing Company, London, 1993
(First edition, Heinemann, 1985)

The Philippines People, Poverty and Politics
Macmillan, London and St Martin's Press, New York, 1987

Revolutionary Struggle in the Philippines
Macmillan, London and St Martin's Press, New York, 1989

Hong Kong and the Asylum-Seekers from Vietnam
Macmillan, London and St Martin's Press, New York, 1991

Social Care: Rivers of Pain, Bridges of Hope
Whiting and Birch Ltd, London, 1992
(First edition, Writers and Publishers Co-operative,
Hong Kong, 1987)

CHILDREN OF THE EAST

LEONARD DAVIS

Reader, Department of Applied Social Studies,
Faculty of Humanities and Social Sciences,
City Polytechnic of Hong Kong

JANUS PUBLISHING COMPANY
London, England

First published in Great Britain 1994
by Janus Publishing Company
Edinburgh House
19 Nassau Street
London W1N 7RE

Copyright © Leonard Davis 1994

**British Library Cataloguing-in-Publication Data.
Davis, Leonard, 1931–
1 Title
Children of the East**

ISBN 1 85756 171 6

All rights reserved. No part of this publication
may be reproduced, stored in a retrieval system or
transmitted in any form or by any means, electronic,
mechanical, photocopying, recording or otherwise,
without the prior permission of the publisher.

The right of Leonard Davis to be identified
as the author of this work has been asserted by
him in accordance with the Copyright Designs
and Patents Act 1988.

Cover design by Harold King

Printed & bound in England by Antony Rowe Ltd,
Chippenham, Wiltshire.

To Liu Ip-wan Philip and Chan Kwok-choi

CONTENTS

	Illustrations	ix
	Preface	xi
	List of Abbreviations	xiii
1	Needs, Rights and Injustices	1
2	Asian Children in Context	5
3	Abuse, Neglect and Disease	25
4	Concern and Intervention	49
	Bibliography	71

ILLUSTRATIONS

Between pages 16 and 17

Plate 1	High school students
Plate 2	Japanese adolescents
Plate 3	Expatriate children
Plate 4	Children in uniform
Plate 5	Boys relaxing
Plate 6	Sports teams
Plate 7	Children performing
Plate 8	The Preda Foundation
Plate 9	Street children begging
Plate 10	Street children
Plate 11	A young beggar in Bangkok
Plate 12	Street children poster
Plates 13 & 14	A rehabilitation centre
Plate 15	Thai-Japanese girl
Plate 16	Chinese-Indian girl
Plate 17	Anglo-Filipino boys
Plate 18	A religious education class
Plate 19	A residential establishment

Between pages 48 and 49

Plate 20	A residential nursery
Plate 21	Handicapped children

Plate 22	A leper colony
Plate 23	Handicapped lead singer
Plate 24	Learning braille
Plate 25	Parental participation
Plate 26	An autistic Korean boy
Plate 27	Early education in Thailand
Plate 28	Widespread acceptance of new ideas
Plate 29	An early afternoon siesta
Plate 30	The author and two young girls
Plate 31	Young boys and commercial enterprise
Plate 32	Children in the fishing industry
Plate 33	Feeding the hungry millions
Plate 34	Attending a wedding
Plate 35	A Buddhist family
Plate 36	A youth worker
Plate 37	Children without childhood
Plate 38	Street families
Plate 39	The spirit of youth

PREFACE

This book is about children in selected countries in Southeast Asia and is based on a research project which was completed in 1993. In many ways, *Children of the East* provides a regional overview – a checklist – targeted not only at those with an academic and professional interest in child care and social policy but also at the concentration of 'successful' people in Southeast Asia and beyond, who on a day-to-day basis are unaffected by the concerns being highlighted and discussed, and remain untouched (intellectually and emotionally) by questions relating to child care policy and practice. The importance of the subject is reinforced by a fact with far-reaching implications, namely, that by the year 2010, 50 per cent of the population of the region will be under 15 years of age.

Many people made this study possible. Key figures in several of the countries under consideration deserve special mention: James Nagayam and Peter Daniel in Malaysia; Yi Bae-Keun in South Korea; Chandraseagran Suppiah and Janey Gilkey in Brunei Darussalam; Breda Noonan, Mary Radcliffe and Shay Cullen in the Philippines; Valerie Emblen in Laos; Elly Sutardjo and Bambang Sentanu in Indonesia; and Orathai Ard-am in Thailand, all of whom provided opportunities for research in Southeast Asia, facilitated my travels in the region and contributed to my understanding. Dr Lornita Wong was the Research Fellow during the first year of the project and made a most valuable contribution. Financial support was given by the University and Polytechnic Grants Committee, Hong Kong, during the period of my appointment as Reader in the Department of Applied Social Studies, and for this I am grateful.

With one exception, that is Plate 12(b), the photographs were taken by the author. They are an integral part of the text and have been chosen both to reflect the main themes of the book and to illuminate some of the more detailed descriptions of daily life, current problems and developmental initiatives. Many children and young people whose pictures are reproduced here have thus made their own individual contributions to the study, as representatives of the millions whose quality of life – whether satisfactory or unsatisfactory – is the subject of this book.

Finally, my thanks are due to Agnes Tsoi of the Department of Applied Social Studies, City Polytechnic of Hong Kong, who worked extremely hard to type and retype several drafts of each chapter, and to meet the final deadline. I would like to acknowledge her considerable help.

LEONARD DAVIS
February 1994

ABBREVIATIONS

AFP	Armed Forces of the Philippines
AIDS	Acquired Immunodeficiency Syndrome
BKKBN	Badan Koordinasi Kelvarga Berencana Nasional
CFC	Child Finding Centre
CRC	Children's Rehabilitation Centre
IUD	Intra-uterine Device
KCF	Korea Children's Foundation
NCIS	National Criminal Intelligence Service
NPA	New People's Army
POSYANDU	Integrated Health Services Stations
PRC	People's Republic of China
SAR	Special Administrative Region
SFPC	State Family Planning Commission
SSR	Stainless Steel Ring
STDs	Sexually-transmitted Diseases
UN	United Nations
UNICEF	United Nations Children's Fund

HIS NAME IS TODAY

We are guilty of many errors and many faults,
but our worst crime is
abandoning the children,
neglecting the fountain of life.
Many of the things we need can wait.
The child cannot.

Right now is the time
his bones are being formed,
his blood is being made
and his senses are being developed.

To him we cannot answer 'Tomorrow'.
His name is 'Today'.

Gabriela Mistral

1

NEEDS, RIGHTS AND INJUSTICES

Over the years, many valuable statements about the rights of children have been developed. Earlier documents were reinforced during the early 1990s by the World Summit for Children (September 1990) and, in December 1990, by the UN Convention on the Rights of the Child. The needs highlighted by such declarations would generally be regarded as universal.

The author has a fundamental belief in the fact that parents – whether married, cohabiting or single – wish to do their best for their children. Generally, those who fail in their task – for example, by distorting the parent–child relationship through incestuous activity; by forcing their offspring into oppressive child labour; by putting their children on the streets to beg or to steal; or by selling their children's bodies for the purpose of prostitution – are most often the victims of their poverty, their own upbringing or their environment.

Moving beyond the need to survive, a great deal is now known about the needs of children: for love and security; for praise and recognition; for support; for personal achievement; and for positive group experience where they can feel free to relax; where they can feel secure, where they can be buttressed by the presence of other people whom they trust; and, most important possibly, where they can obtain continual reassurance in regard to their identity (Caplan, 1969). In subscribing to and thinking about global declarations – worthy and welcome as they are – it is important always to remember the 12-year-old boy from Bangkok who looks like a six-year old. With his father dead and his mother a prostitute, he lives on the streets, sniffing glue and begging.

Most children of poor parents remain poor; many children who live in residential institutions later become the parents of children who live in instititions. Readers familiar with the concept of the 'cycle of deprivation' will know exactly what is meant. A major fear for the future must be that with, at best, a constant level of educational and welfare services provision, such a cycle of deprivation will too easily slide into a 'spiral of deprivation'. While it may be possible to break into a cycle of deprivation, the consequences of failing to arrest a spiral of deprivation are awesome. Deprivation accelerates as those least affected distance themselves from the powerlessness of large groups of men, women and children. The empowerment of the deprived is, therefore, a topic about which there should always be concern.

Within the framework of the more traditional responses to children, some individual projects in the region known to the author – both in government and voluntary sectors – have generated extremely positive feelings regarding well-planned work, perceptive needs assessment, often adequate facilities, appropriate geographical locations, well-motivated (and sometimes trained or partly-trained) staff, strong parental involvement and competent leadership and management. In South Korea, the author is thinking of some excellent day centres and a specialist residential unit for severely handicapped children managed sympathetically by a leading voluntary organisation; in Japan, of the development of an assessment unit in Tokyo staffed by skilled professionals; in Laos, of daycare centres attached to government departments and of the initiatives of one visiting expatriate; in Hong Kong, of the well-baby clinics and playgroups in some of the detention centres and refugee camps; in Singapore and Malaysia, of the enthusiastic staff in child care settings, both management and grassroots workers; in Brunei, of some of the specialist work

Needs, Rights and Injustices 3

undertaken with handicapped children; and, in the Philippines, of drop-in centres for street children, and the Children's Rehabilitation Centres in Manila and elsewhere, facilities which cater basically for the child victims of war.

In the south of the Philippines, on the island of Mindanao, the author also spent time at the House of Friendship. This was a hard mud, open courtyard surrounded by a collection of tightly packed, single-storey buildings, serving a variety of purposes and bordered by a six-foot wall, and the home of the most mixed group of 50 or more people – young, very young and old – ever seen by the author in one residential establishment: four members of one family, all blind as a result of dietary deficiency; a 70-year-old woman sitting silently; young girls at risk; little orphaned boys; and a blind, phyically handicapped infant trying to make sense of his environment by exploration and touch.

Under the verandah were two six-week-old babies in wooden boxes with three layers of muslin cloth over the top as a protection against mosquitoes. One young man, his legs amputated below the knees and with minimal eyesight, edged his way along a concrete path, sweeping it carefully with a small brush. A number of volunteer workers assisted the Filipino Catholic sister in charge of the House of Friendship, who took time to sit with the author in the centre of the courtyard in order to talk about the people being cared for. In spite of the abject poverty, there was beauty. The dignity of each person was being preserved. This preservation of individual dignity was also found in many of the projects referred to above.

2
ASIAN CHILDREN IN CONTEXT

As noted in the Preface, this book is based on a research project which was essentially a 'quality of life' study about children in selected countries in Southeast Asia. Overall, the project aimed to examine various social indicators such as infant mortality, family size and life expectancy before considering, for example, questions relating to family care; educational opportunities; handicapped children; deprived and delinquent children; street children; refugee children; child abuse and neglect; child labour; child prostitution; residential/institutional care (the preferred term is 'residential care' but reference is made most frequently by the general public to children in institutions); and urban/rural variations.

As the study progressed, the powerful effects of poverty on children and young people became increasingly apparent, together with the emergence of sharp images of the paths to which these phenomena will lead around the turn of the century. This poverty goes well beyond the traditional notions associated with hunger – and, indeed, the widespread starvation which continues to exist – and is additionally concerned with emotional, social and physical neglect and abuse, against a background of children's rights.

The statistical picture presented in Tables 2.1 and 2.2 provides a background to the countries on which this book is focused. The picture is not immediately encouraging. Some figures – for instance, those relating to school pupil populations – give an indication of the size of the task. The 1991 population figures for children under 15 years of age are also illuminating: 22 per cent of the total population in Hong Kong; 24 per cent in Singapore; 37 per cent in Malaysia; 40 per cent in Indonesia; and 39 per cent in Vietnam. While it will take 99 years for the number of people in Hong Kong (population of 5.7 million) to double; and 133 years in the case of Japan, the 63 million people in the Philippines will take only 27 years to reach more than 126 million. The population of Hong Kong may, of course, be affected from 1997 onwards when the territory becomes a Special Administrative Region (SAR) of mainland China, if, for example, people from the People's Republic of China (PRC) come flooding in from rural areas across the border.

Table 2.1

	Per capita income (US$)	Under-five mortality rate (per 1000)	Life expectancy (years)
Japan	25,273	8	79
Brunei	15,200	12*	71
Hong Kong	12,068	10	77
Singapore	11,245	12	73
Taiwan	7,332	17*	74
Macau	8,100	11*	77
Malaysia	2,297	32	68
South Korea	5,569	33	71
Thailand	7,332	49	65
North Korea	987	33	69
Philippines	865	73	64
Indonesia	560	119	61
China	298	43	68
Vietnam	200*	88	63
Laos	156	159	50
Cambodia	190	199	49

* estimate

Source: Per capita income and life expectancy, Asia Yearbook, 1992, Far Eastern Economic Review, 1991
Under-five mortality rate, UNICEF Facts and Figures, 1990

Table 2.2

	Population 1991 (m)	Population Year 2010 (m)	Years until population doubles	% under 15 years (1991)	Infant mortality rate per 1000 (1991)	Primary students	Secondary students
Brunei	0.3	0.4	27	36	7.0	36,983	18,748
Burma	42.1	51.6	36	38	103.0	5.42m	1.26m
China	1087.0	1151.3	48	27	44.0	122.42m	51.05m
Hong Kong	5.7	6.3	99	22	7.4	524,919	431,381
Indonesia	177.4	213.7	41	40	73.0	29.66m	10.09m
Japan	122.7	130.0	133	21	4.5	9.16m	5.19m
Cambodia	6.7	8.5	32	35	125.0	919,500	98,800
North Korea	21.8	28.5	39	29	30.0	n.a.	n.a.
South Korea	42.6	48.8	79	30	23.0	4.70m	4.40m
Laos	3.8	5.0	32	43	124.0	495,375	69,226
Macau	0.4	0.5	41	23	10.0	32,639	16,862
Malaysia	17.0	20.9	28	37	29.0	2.45m	1.30m
Philippines	63.2	85.5	27	39	54.0	10.28m	3.90m
Singapore	2.6	2.9	55	24	6.6	257,932	161,029
Taiwan	19.8	22.4	62	27	6.2	2.35m	1.93m
Thailand	54.7	66.4	40	34	29.0	6.96m	2.23m
Vietnam	65.2	86.0	31	39	44.0	n.a.	n.a.

n.a. not available

Source: *Asia Yearbook*, 1992 (*Far Eastern Economic Review*, 1991)

There are particular worries throughout the region: the high levels of sexual exploitation of children; the intense pollution in inner cities; and the flight of people from the countryside to the towns. By the year 2010, the population of Manila will increase from 8 million to 11.2 million; Jakarta will move from 9.4 million to 13.3 million; and Bangkok-Thonburi's population from 7.2 million to 10.5 million. The costs of providing new health, educational and welfare services are high, and the space not always available in the urban areas. The web of inner city difficulties, already complex and confusing, will inevitably grow. For many young people, the school curriculum is irrelevant, with pressures to achieve, regardless of the emotional cost, within the framework of over-formal, unyielding, often unsympathetic systems, which detract from the joy of learning and make unnatural demands on children and young people. This appears especially so in the case of younger adolescents, but does occur throughout the age range; and in primary, secondary and tertiary education.

In terms of 'quality of life' and apart from what must be the major concerns in the region – for example, infant mortality, child labour and child prostitution – there are other issues, some localised, some regional, to which attention should be paid, for instance, to refugees in the region: the internal refugees in the Philippines; and the Vietnamese in Hong Kong and elsewhere. In Hong Kong alone, among the thousands of children held in detention centres, there were in 1991, 2500 'unaccompanied minors' who never left their wire enclosures. In one detention centre, some children were held in a secure hut within the perimeter fence, a significant comment on one of the tragic events that happened during the final phase of British colonial rule. Thailand, too, incarcerated thousands of children and young people in its refugee camps. Many of these children in Hong Kong and Thailand had been witness to numerous incidents of violence. In Hong Kong, many children were caught up in tear-gas attacks. On the Thai-Cambodian border, they were shelled by forces in Cambodia. Children at sea – on their way from Vietnam to Hong Kong with their families as 'boat people' – had the most horrific stories to tell about pirates, rape, violence and murder.

Needing special concern are children who live in residential homes and residential schools. While, in most cases, the food they receive appears to be adequate for their physical needs, the quality of their emotional lives is often woefully inadequate. It is not too difficult to find rows and rows of tiny children in large wards, without stimulation and without individual care. Theoretical knowledge about the needs of children in their early years is thus contradicted in practice. Without mother/child or substitute mother/child bonding, these children become the parents of children who start life in the same way in the next generation.

Residential homes for older children, too, are often equally open to criticism, although several examples of good practice are to be found in Chapter 4. While appreciating the historical and cultural legacies which appear to encourage the development of large residential units – in Japan, South Korea, the Philippines and elsewhere – it is essential to consider the quality of life in these establishments, where, quite frequently, children have no experience of 'being parented' in the traditional sense. The development of the 'emotional self' is thus seriously impaired. The expansion of foster homes – for instance, in Japan, South Korea and Hong Kong – does not appear to have occurred to the extent necessary and possible.

Within Southeast Asia, many countries are not even in sight of the level of social, educational and welfare services required to cater for today's child population; too few people are anticipating in practical terms what the level of need will be in the year 2000 and beyond; and only the tiniest fraction of the adult population in Southeast Asia appears actively involved in programme planning, policy formulation and the development of child care action packages. Relatively few inroads are, therefore, being made into the range of injustices facing children who, fortunately or unfortunately, happen to have been born in this part of the world; 'fortunately' because, overall – apart from some of the highest levels of malnutrition it is possible to find – the problems of Southeast Asia do not seem as great as those found in some other parts of the globe, for example, in Africa and certain South American, Middle Eastern and East European countries. For that reason, the difficulties in Southeast Asia appear to have a hope of at least partial resolution. Children in the region, however, remain 'unfortunate' because the difficulties are widespread; the burdens imposed on children in most countries in Southeast Asia are far more than they should be expected to carry; and, without greater determination on the part of adults, are likely to get worse.

Individual country reports about the state of child care – most often produced by the governments themselves – refer, positively and with optimism, to progress in the development of services, and in statistical terms frequently identify fewer difficulties in particular problem areas. Such reports are encouraging, bearing in mind that certain emphases and omissions are clearly political in nature. In some instances, with the help of international organisations, real inroads are being made against childhood diseases. On the other hand, the failure to fight some major ills – and, indeed, to see them increase in some areas – indicates that many battles are far from being won.

POPULATION GROWTH

According to *Family Health International*, at least 1.3 billion babies will be born between now and the end of the century, more births than in any previous decade in human history. At the same time, the final decade of the 20th century may witness the deaths of 170–180 million infants and children, if mortality levels remain the same as in the 1980s. This means that about 50 000 infants and children will die every day.

In general, about half of all childhood deaths under the age of five occur during the first year of life. Potts and Thapa report in the *Family Health International* publication that half to two-thirds of all infant deaths take place within four weeks of birth. Fortunately, knowledge and technologies are available to prevent a significant proportion of these deaths. For some years now, GOBI (growth monitoring, oral rehydration therapy, breastfeeding and immunisation) has been pursued as a comprehensive strategy for improving infant and child mortality statistics world-wide. These interventions continue to play a critical role in primary health care for children, and are practised extensively throughout many countries in Southeast Asia.

Over 95 per cent of the world's infant deaths occur every year in developing countries: 0.3 million (2.7 per cent) in the developed world; 3 million (27.7 per cent) in Africa; 0.8 million (7.6 per cent) in Latin America; 0.8 million (7.6 per cent) in China; and 5 million (45.7 per cent) in Asia. It is estimated that during the period 1990 to 1994, more than 50 million births will occur in developing countries. Potts and Thapa go on to suggest that an equally important component in reducing infant and child mortality is family planning, stating: 'Family planning targets couples; child survival interventions target infants and children. Both are primary health interventions and can contribute to lowering the number of infant and child deaths.'

FAMILY PLANNING

With few exceptions, family planning programmes are found throughout the countries of Southeast Asia. Even with their huge populations, Thailand and Indonesia may be considered among the leaders of the region in population control.

Thailand

Recognising that population growth would have serious implications for the nation's future development, a national family planning policy was advocated in Thailand in the 1960s and became a reality in 1970 when the Cabinet approved the adoption of a national policy on population growth and family planning with the objective of reducing the rate of increase from over 3.0 per cent to 2.5 per cent per year in a five-year period. After the 1970–75 period, the objective was then shifted to a goal of 2.0 per cent for the five-year period beginning in 1976. This policy also included two subsidiary goals: (i) to limit family size through voluntary family planning; and (ii) to enhance the status of maternal and child health care.

One of the most important studies about Thailand was prepared by Aphichat Chamratrithirong, Bencha Yoddumnern-Attig and Orapin Singhadej of Mahidol University: *The Effect of Reduced Family Size on the Status of Maternal and Child Health*. The specific aims of the study were (i) to investigate the status of maternal and child health in two distinct groups of women of smaller families and of larger ones, in two regions of Thailand – the North where fertility had been declining significantly and the South where fertility had just begun to decline, on a more moderate basis; (ii) to compare and assess the status of maternal health in two groups of women, that is, contraceptive and non-contraceptive users in the North and the South; (iii) to investigate the accessibility and use of family planning services in the two distinct groups of women, namely, women of smaller families and of larger ones, in the North and the South; (iv) to compare the effect of reduced family size on maternal and child health in the two groups of women, that is, women of smaller families and of larger ones, in the North and the South; and (v) to compare the health and economic rationale of family planning practice in both the northern and southern regions.

In the research project, five villages were selected from Nan province in the South and six from Chiengrai province in the North. In the southern region, villages were selected from the provinces of Phang-Nga, where five villages were chosen, and from Songkla, where twelve villages were studied. A total of 28 villages were thus included in the project.

The findings of the study showed that the knowledge and use of family planning were widespread in the two regions under consideration, especially among the northern women. Knowledge of selected contraceptive methods was almost universal. Approximately 76 per cent of women in the North were using some form of contraception and an additional 13 per cent had, on occasions, used some form of contraception. Only about 11 per cent of the married women in the reproductive age never used any means of contraception. Comparable data was found for the South. The level of current contraceptive use was clearly lower in the South, and the majority of 'ever-married' women practised contraception as early as when they were 15 to 19 years old. The most popular methods used was female sterilisation (45.0 per cent in the North, 30.8 per cent in the South); and the second most popular method was oral pills which accounted for 31.8 per cent in the North and 28.4 per cent in the South. Injectables were found to be comparatively popular among northern women in contrast to their counterparts in the South. On the contrary, withdrawal and rhythm methods accounted for as high as 16.3 per cent and 9.5 per cent respectively among contraceptive users in the South whereas in the North none reported withdrawal as a method used and less than 1 per cent used a rhythm method. Vasectomy was practised by 6 per cent in the South. Other methods were much less popular. None reported the use of sub-dermal implants. Condoms and vaginal methods were found to be rare.

In general, findings on method popularity (and/or availability) supported other studies in Thailand, namely, that sterilisation had become the most common method followed closely by the Pill. Injections were common in the North where a long history of injectable use was known. Prevalence of withdrawal in the South was, according to the researchers, not surprising and confirmed its popularity as found in earlier studies. The underlying factor of its popularity was also related to both religious teachings and the way of life in the South.

Women in the sample were asked when they first thought of using birth control methods. As only about 6 per cent of all women, in both regions, never considered using any form of family planning, it became apparent that the concept of contraception was quite well established among these women. A considerable number of women who had fewer pregnancies, and were probably younger, had thought about family planning methods very early. This may reflect the fact that family planning methods are used for spacing as well as limiting, especially among the new generation of women. In both North and South the timing of the first thoughts about family planning was quite similar. Approximately 20 per cent in both samples had begun thinking of contraception before marriage or the first pregnancy. The majority of women in both samples felt that contraception had no effect on their health.

In summary, contraception was well accepted by both samples although the method was different. Northern women had high rates of use and relied on more modern methods of contraception than their southern counterparts. Overall, both samples of women had sufficient knowledge and experience with contraception to take advantage of it to meet their desired family size.

Indonesia

At more than 180 million at the beginning of 1992, Indonesia ranks as the world's fifth most populous nation, after China, India, the Commonwealth of Independent States (formerly the Soviet Union) and the United States of America. A population growth policy has been in operation in Indonesia since 1967, with a family planning programme being included in each five-year development plan. Initially, a National Family Planning Institute was established, with the status of a quasi-governmental agency. The institute developed the national family planning programme and managed its funds. In 1970, the status of the institute was upgraded to the National Family Planning Coordinating Boad (NFPCB) – *Badan Koordinasi Kelvarga Berencana Nasional* (BKKBN).

In the First Five-year Development Plan, the family planning programme covered six provinces on the islands of Java and Bali; Jakarta, West Java, Central Java, Togyakarta, East Java and Bali. In the Second Five-Year Development Plan, the programme was extended to include ten additional provinces in the outer islands, including Aceh, North Sumatra, West Sumatra, South Sumatra, Lampung, South Kalimantan, North Sulawesi and South Sulawesi provinces. With the Third Five-Year Development Plan, the programme was extended to all 27 provinces of Indonesia.

Rapid population growth together with unbalanced population and age distribution have long been the main problems in the area of population facing Indonesian national development. In order to solve these problems, the First Five-year Development Plan (1967–72) included efforts implemented through the national family planning programme to reduce population growth and to improve welfare, especially mother and child welfare. This was emphasised on 8 June 1989 by President Soeharto at the United Nations Population Award Presentation Ceremony when he said:

> ... the Family Planning programme forms part of an effort towards nation building to fight poverty, backwardness and indifference. Family Planning is neither a purely quantitative demographic matter nor a clinical matter of contraception, but it involves an endeavour to bring about changes in the value system and norms.

The family planning programme that initially needed a persistent persuasive campaign, which was practically conducted door-to-door, has begun to become a movement of self-reliant family planning. The traditional belief extolling large families with many children is now changing into a small, happy and prosperous family norm ... The family planning programme introduced new ideas which were not entirely congruent with the norms that for many centuries, from generation to generation, had been deeply rooted in our society. In a traditional agricultural community, every child is a source of happiness: each would bring good fortune, providing help to fathers in the fields and to mothers in the kitchens, and comfort to parents in dealing with the hardships of life. In such a community it would never occur to anyone that each child is also a burden and the source of difficulties in the life of the family. It would be even more unthinkable for them to conceive the idea that the total number of children in all families throughout the country would impose a burden on the entire nation. Most of the people, with their limited knowledge, could not even imagine that they could really control their living conditions – even less their life expectancy – through a healthier way of life and more mature family planning. Obviously there existed a wide gap in the people's thinking that had to be bridged before we could even start with the programme.

The gap has been successfully bridged. This, I believe, was due to the role played by the guardians of socio-cultural norms who were trusted by the community, such as religious leaders and other prominent members of the community. They served as reminders to us all that children are not the property of parents, to be considered merely as guarantors for old age, but God has entrusted them to us 'temporarily' and they become the responsibility of each set of parents, to be raised and educated, so that they become responsible and self-reliant individuals. As far as our society was concerned, which generally holds very strong

High school students in a park in South Korea.

Japanese adolescents visiting a shrine in Tokyo.

Expatriate children in Hong Kong and Singapore are generally privileged.

Children throughout the region are attracted to uniformed organisations.

Boys relaxing in the grounds of Chulalongkorn University, Bangkok.

Sports teams are formed whenever groups get together. This picture was also taken in the grounds of Chulalongkorn University.

Children performing at one of the numerous regional seminars that take place on a regular basis.

A principal concern of the Preda Foundation is its work with street children, and those who have been sexually abused.

Street children beg outside the clubs and bars in Olongapo city, Philippines.

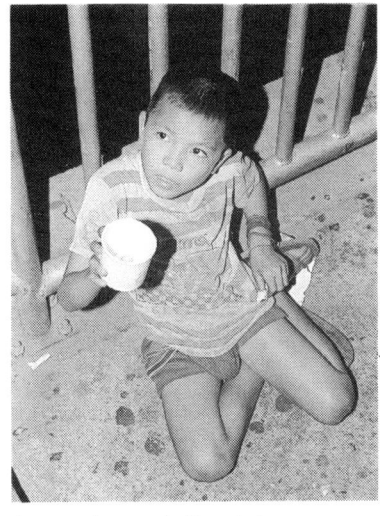

Many street children never attend school, and have inadequate nutrition and health care.

When the pain of poverty is too much to bear a marginalized generation appears.

Help the 3,000 Abandoned & Street Children of Olongapo attain a just and humane living condition.

CONTACT:
- SOR EVA PALENCIA, DC
  ST. JOSEPH COMMUNITY CENTER
  OLONGAPO CITY - Phone 222-4031
- MS. JUANITA LAFORTEZA
  MSSD, OLONGAPO CITY
  Phone 222-2910
- DR. GENEROSO E. ESPINOSA
  CITY HEALTH OFFICER
  OLONGAPO CITY - Phone 222-4123
- JEROME CALUYO
  222-4122

PRINTED BY NEWLIFE VISIONS

A young beggar in Bangkok.

The Philippines and Thailand seem to have more street children than any other country in the region.

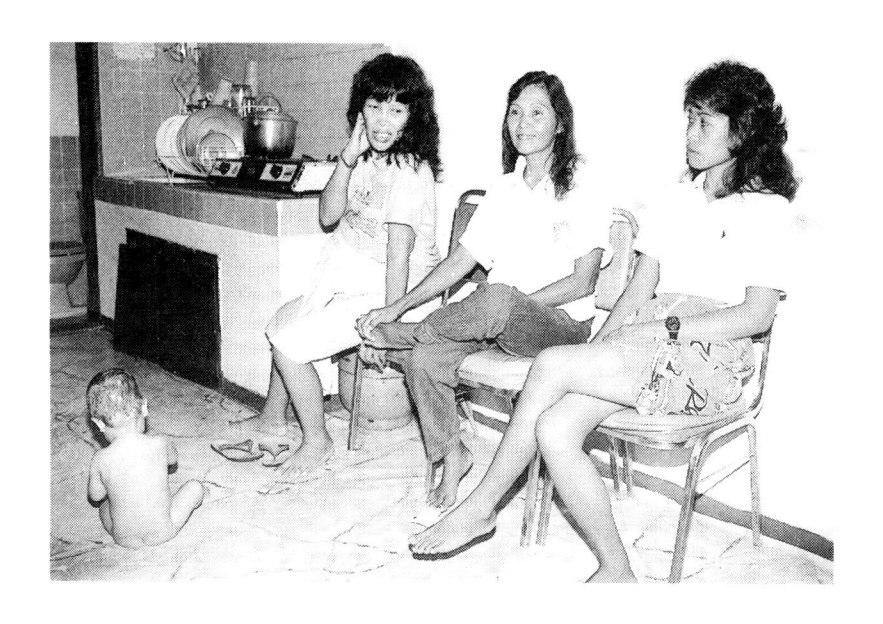

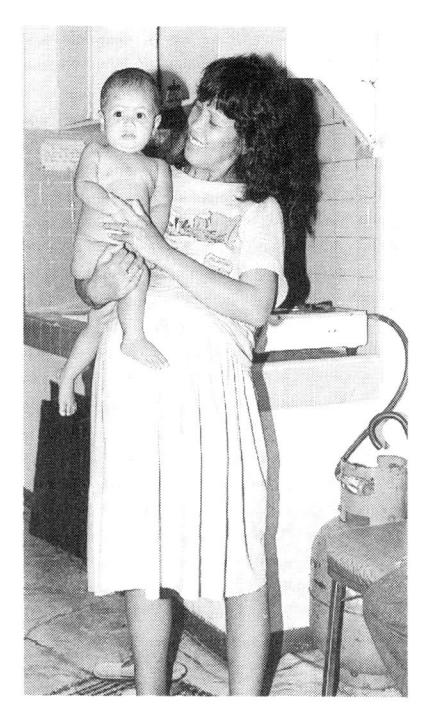

These pictures were taken in the Philippines: at a rehabilitation centre for former prostitutes and their young children.

This girl's mother comes from Thailand. Her father is Japanese.

This girl from Singapore is of Chinese-Indian parentage.

These Anglo-Filipino boys, Michael and Christopher, are the sons of the author.

A religious education class in a girls' remand home in Malaysia.

These children live in an attractive, well-run residential establishment in Malaysia.

religious views, such an idea constituted a breakthrough that opened the way for family planning.

The successful implementation of the programme depended mainly on the dedication of fieldworkers and the participation of various social groups and organisations. One of the most effective types of participation was in the form of activities at the village level. There are now currently no less than 200 000 rural institutions such as Acceptor Groups, Family Welfare Promotion Groups, Integrated Health Services Stations (POSYANDU) and other active organisations. These formed the spearheads of the family planning programme that reach the community, from urban areas to village levels and remote areas.

The State Policy Guidelines, issued by the 1973 People's Consultative Assembly, declared that the objective of the national family planning programme during the Second Five-Year Development Plan period was to improve maternal and child health in order to create, as noted in President Soeharto's speech, a small, happy and prosperous family norm. The 1988 State Policy Guidelines added that the national family planning programme should also be directed at reducing mortality rates.

As already noted, family planning programme implementation throughout Indonesia's various regions has been gradually accomplished over a period of 20 years. The First Development plan covered those regions with a large population, namely, Java and Bali. Coverage was enlarged during the Second Five-Year Plan leading to overall coverage in Indonesia by the National Family Planning Programme.

According to Nancy and David Piet, nowhere in Indonesia has community involvement with family planning been more evident, or more effective, than in Bali. Several thousand community organisations have assisted in changing Bali from one of Indonesia's most humanly fertile provinces to its least fertile. In 1971, the average number of births per woman was just under six; by 1976 – in short, five years later – the average number of births per woman was down to 3.8, representing a reduction of more than one-third.

Nancy and David Piet suggested that, at the heart of these changes, were 3708 Balinese community organisations (*banjars*) which have transformed the population programme in Bali into a community movement, providing a model for other parts of Indonesia and possibly the world. In *Family Planning and the Banjars of Bali*, Nancy and David Piet explain the *banjar* organisation and structure:

> The *Banjars* are both the basic residential settlements in the Balinese countryside and the traditional community grouping within these settlements for cooperative and ceremonial activity. The origins of the *banjars* have been clouded by the centuries but they have survived as extraordinarily strong social and administrative groups. Today they function as cooperative societies of people obliged to help each other physically and morally.
>
> The key to the *banjars* lies in the distinctive socio-religious structure of Balinese society. Bali is an enclave of essentially Hindu culture in an otherwise Moslem region. There is a system of social stratification derived from the Indian caste system, to which the Balinese have added their own system of social groupings based on kinship and generations (descent through the male line, that is, father-son-grandson). The patrilineal kin ties overlap with a system of inherited titles and link most Balinese to a kinship organisation, the *dadia*, whose members have all inherited the same title through the male line and live in the same *banjar*. The *dadia* has its own temple, influences membership of political parties and may specialise in such work as forging instruments for the *gamelan* – the Balinese orchestra consisting of chimes and gongs. The BKKBN hoped to improve follow-up and record keeping by involving the *banjars*. As communities became more aware of birth con-

trol issues it was hoped that *banjar* members would help each other deal with side effects, identify potential acceptors and generally make family planning part of their own activities.

The plan worked. In mid-1975, Dr Ida Bagus Attawa, Chairman of the Bali BKKBN, extended the training to 400 more *banjars*. The programme developed rapidly and by the end of 1976 a surprisingly large target had been reached. All 3708 *banjars* in 564 villages had become involved with the family planning programme. By 1977, the figures being returned to the family planning offices were also indicating impressive trends. It was estimated that 60 per cent of couples where the woman was in the reproductive age group (15–44 years of age) were registered as family planning acceptors – compared to an Indonesian average of 30 per cent. The most visible sign of acceptance is still seen on the *banjar* map which is prominently displayed on the wall of the *bale banjar* (meeting hall) at the monthly *banjar* meeting. The house of every eligible couple is clearly marked on the map to show whether or not they are family planning acceptors. If a couple is using contraception their house is further marked and a colour code indicates which method is being used: blue for IUDs, red for the Pill, and green for the condom. The map also indicates if residents are newly married or if the woman is pregnant. It is supplemented by a detailed register, which records information essential for evaluating and monitoring the whole family planning programme: names, wife's age, date of acceptance, number of children and monthly contraceptive status. Any change in this status can be seen at a glance and the couple approached by other members of the *banjar*, the family planning fieldworker or the nurse-midwife. An up-to-date register is kept and a quarterly report sent to the BKKBN office.

While kinship is the essential qualification for the *dadia*, for the *banjar* it is residence and sex. Membership of the *banjar* organistion is compulsory for all married men. An average *banjar* has 600 members, and an average village, as Nancy and David Piet state, will have five or six *banjars*. Residential land is owned and allocated by the *banjar*, which also organises a range of mutual help and ceremonial activities. Thus the *banjars* organise unpaid labour for community maintenance work and lend money to needy members, particularly for the elaborate cremation ceremonies. In effect, *banjars* control most day-to-day aspects of religious and community life. The Piets continue:

> Failure to attend the *banjar* meeting or to carry out appointed duties, involves a fine of either rice or money. If anyone fails to join the *banjar* after receiving three invitations it is assumed that he has deliberately refused to comply. He is then declared morally and socially 'dead', boycotted from all community activity and even denied the right to have his remains buried in the local cemetery.

As Nancy and David Piet sum up:

> There is no question that bringing family planning to the *banjar* has brought success in family planning ... Bali will undoubtedly face some hard years before the population comes into balance with available land and resources. But hopefully the spirit of cooperation and concern of the Balinese for each other and the good of the community will keep them on the path as they struggle to retain control over their destiny.

China

Now that the Cultural Revolution baby-boom generation is moving beyond its peak reproductive years, the PRC has entered a critical phase in controlling population growth. Since 1986, 12–13 million young women have been reaching childbearing age each year, and this rate will continue until about 1997.

Fertile women aged between 15 and 44 now make up more than a quarter of China's total population, estimated at more than 1.1 billion. At the current 14.2 per thousand rate of natural increase, China's population will increase by another 10 per cent every seven years, presenting a family planning problem of awesome dimensions.

China has in recent years failed to achieve its policy goal of one child per family, while ineffective contraceptives have played a major role in the country recording what is estimated as the sixth highest abortion rate in the world – about 40 per 1000 women aged between 15 and 44. Robert Delfs has reported that about 70 per cent of the estimated 11 million abortions carried out each year in China were due to contraceptive failure, according to state family planning officials. The failure rate of the most widely used method of contraception in China – an intra-uterine device (IUD) known as the stainless steel ring (SSR) – is at least 10 per cent, and may be as high as 15 per cent. Commonly used IUDs in developed countries have a failure rate of only 1 per cent.

More reliable IUDs are manufactured in China, but the cost of a locally-made copper-T IUD is about Rmb 1.40 (30 US cents). While this price is modest, China's large population of fertile women requires about 12 million new IUD insertions each year. Each SSR costs only Rmb 0.10.

The additional funds needed for better IUDs would be only a fraction of the costs of carrying out approximately 7–8 million unnecessary abortions ever year. But, as Delfs says, in China, the State Family Planning Commission (SFPC) is separate from (and technically outranks) the Ministry of Public Health. SFPC funds pay for the IUDs supplied free in family planning clinics throughout the country. However, the commission does not have to pay for the abortions needed when its SSR IUDs fail. At the grassroots level, demand for the copper-T has grown quickly as the inadequacy of the SSR device has become better known, and the manufacturers of high-quality IUDs are increasingly bypassing the SFPC in Peking and selling directly to local government clinics and family planning organisations.

Illegal births in defiance of the state's policies, especially in rural areas, total about nine million each year – more than a third of all births. One SFPC survey reported that, between 1980 and 1987, the average Chinese family had 2.47 children.

SFPC officials reportedly told Delfs that cases of forced abortion and sterilisation highlighted in the foreign press were isolated incidents which violated state policies. This may currently be the case but in 1982–3 it is believed that there were millions of mandatory abortions and sterilisations. The strong public reaction to the extremely harsh enforcement of family planning regulations during this period was an important factor in promoting the relatively more humane policy adopted the following year, which allows exemptions for a wide range of special cases.

The 1982–3 crackdown came in response to an unexpected surge in the natural birth rate in 1981–2, which may have been related to rural decollectivisation and the associated weakening of the party's rural control apparatus.

The dimensions of the problem did not become clear until the results of preliminary surveys for the 1982 census became available. These figures may have triggered the authorities' responses: central party document number 11 of 1982 was, as Delfs reports, seemingly a stern admonition to local leaders for losing control of family planning.

The number of abortions rose from 8.7 million in 1981 to 12.4 million in 1982 to 14.4 million in 1983. The most striking feature of the 1982–3 crackdown was the number of sterilisations – more than 16 million in 1983 alone, compared with 3.9 million the previous year.

Abortion and sterilisation orders are enforced mainly through the threat of fines, rather than the use of force. Delfs refers to the case of a peasant and his wife who had already had an illegal second child in 1981, and ran away from their county after receiving an order to submit to an abortion. On returning with their third child, the couple was fined Rmb 250 for the birth of the second child and Rmb 600 for the third child, neither of whom would be allotted contractual land in their village. The couple was also ordered to give up a piece of land they had contracted to farm, and charged a child-raising fee of Rmb 10 per month, to be paid from the beginning of pregnancy of the third child until it reached the age of 14. The wife was ordered to submit to tubal ligation, and a fine of Rmb 10 imposed for each day from the issuance of the notice until the operation.

In China, the population's rates of natural increase vary regionally from lows of 6–10 per thousand in the municipalities of Peking, Tianjin and Shanghai to 16–19 per thousand in Yunnan, Guizhou, Ningxia and Tibet. These are all minority areas where strict population control measures had not previously been enforced, although this policy is now being changed. Delfs reported that, among predominantly Han provinces, Annhui, Hunan and Guangdong have recorded increased rates in excess of 15 per thousand. Guangdong also has the highest multiple birth rate for a predominantly Han province.

Population control – whether by education as in Indonesia (and to a lesser extent in Thailand) or by enforcement as in China – remains one of the keys to child care problems in Southeast Asia. The competing countries in the region can neither feed nor educate the vast numbers of children and young people who populate them, and there is insufficient funding for the levels of health care, education and social welfare programmes which the ever-growing numbers of children have a right to expect. Regulating the 'chance to be born' of many children is, for many people, a sad option, a consideration which manifests itself most forcibly as one mixes with Asian children from a range of countries and sees and experiences their individual potential, their charm and their skills, together with their natural abilities to communicate and to learn. Foreign aid cannot forever be depended upon as the source of a nation's progress in child care. The implementation of some of the recommendations made at the end of Chapter 4 – in seeking a way out of the impasse – may provide a sense of direction for the early part of the 21st century, especially in the face of the fact that, by the year 2010 (and probably beyond) 50 per cent of the population of the region will be under 15 years of age. As the quotation from President Soeharto's speech stated – and this would probably apply to many countries in the region – essential developments in the field of population control can only be brought about as a result of major changes in well-rooted 'value systems and norms'.

3
ABUSE, NEGLECT AND DISEASE

By most criteria, the outlook for the majority of Asian children is gloomy. As millions struggle for life itself, Asian children make up the daily count of 20 000 world-wide who die from preventable diseases; of 100 000 who become undernourished; and of 115 000 who drop out of primary school.

Others in the region flee from their homes in terror while thousands have their limbs and bodies torn apart by the weapons of war, or experience a premature death as a result of neglect, sexual abuse or exploitation as cheap labour.

For Asian children as a whole, the world is at best inhospitable and, for very many, cruel and destructive. Only in a select number of countries in the region, Hong Kong and Singapore included, do children have some protection from the most abusive attacks on their physical and emotional beings. The plight of children elsewhere in the region – mutilated, exploited, bought, sold and rented for the attractiveness of their flesh (for example, in Thailand and the Philippines) – is a problem that most people cannot bear to confront.

Unless, however, the issues are raised and tackled now, the destruction of young lives and the premature deaths of many others will have become so common by the turn of the century that adults will be faced with the most horrifying statistics, reflecting even deeper man's inhumanity to children. The plight of children in Asia is a tragic problem that must be approached with a degree of urgency, for the future of the region depends upon the young.

Some research and understanding from the West – for instance, in respect of the significance of mother–child relationships, the care of children with physical and mental disabilities, and children's rights – is necessary.

Of greater importance, however, is finding Asian solutions to Asian problems, an approach that is already paying dividends, given the limited resources available. In comparison with the West, the antecedents of the countries in the region are most often different, and the size of the problems is different. Within Asia, the variations from country to country are stark. Each country has its individual and specific difficulties, and its peculiar ways of tackling them. Only some issues are universal. Undoubtedly, there are common problems: for instance (i) among children living in isolated rural communities – for example, in Thailand, the Philippines, Indonesia, Vietnam and Laos (with the parallel effects of poverty being a unifying factor); (ii) among children living in rapidly-developing urbanised communities – for example, in Japan, Hong Kong, Taiwan, South Korea and Singapore (with over-intensive educational systems and excessive child-indulgence, associated with inappropriate and exaggerated consumerism, as noticeable features); (iii) among street children – for example, in Thailand, Malaysia and the Philippines (where prostitution all too frequently provides an additional source of income); (iv) among children having to leave their homes, for example, in Cambodia, Vietnam and the Philippines (where, in the first two countries they have been forced to flee to Thailand and Hong Kong respectively, and in the last, as internal refugees, they have suffered extensively as a result of the continuing conflict between government military forces and the New People's Army; and (v) among children who have received little or no protection from some of the worst diseases, namely, those that are sexually transmitted (especially AIDS), poliomyelitis, tuberculosis, malaria, schistosomiasis and leprosy, some of which, as noted above, stem directly from the widespread poverty found throughout the region.

Abuse, Neglect and Disease 27

Problems faced by children in relation to AIDS are not, of course, confined to children in developing countries. Even though, for example, those living in Hong Kong and Singapore may have a high level of protection from most diseases as a result of almost universal vaccination programmes, the possibility of becoming infected with AIDS has remained as high as in any other western-type community. In March 1993 there were an estimated 26 HIV positive children attending Hong Kong schools, all haemophiliacs infected by the transfusion of contaminated blood or blood products. So great was the scare that the Education Department issued a circular in the same month, stating that children seriously injured at school would not receive any help from teachers until the teachers had protected themselves with disposable plastic gloves. Issued on behalf of the Director of Education, the memorandum stated that such precautions as wearing disposable gloves when handling wounds, and avoiding contact with blood should be followed 'at all times'.

While acknowledging that staff members in schools require as much protection as children in the fight against AIDS, in policy terms, the way in which the Hong Kong government is even able to approach the problem (through its circular) highlights yet one more discrepancy between rich and poor Asian countries; as hundreds die of a disease in one country, a privileged group a few hundred miles away are given levels of protection that may safeguard their very existence.

Shortly after the publication of the Hong Kong Education Department circular, in March 1993, the government unveiled details of a HK$350 million AIDS grant, the sum to include a $100 million compassionate grant, $200 million for medical support services and $50 million for prevention programmes.

The $100 million ex-gratia payment to Hong Kong's 61 HIV-infected haemophiliacs and their families included the 26 schoolboys already mentioned above and the families of five who had already died of AIDS, the latter having been believed to have been infected when they were injected with contaminated blood before screening tests were introduced in 1985. Such sophistication and comparative generosity present no major financial difficulties to a territory like Hong Kong, thereby providing relief to hundreds of individuals and families, but again reinforces the inequalities of life between what will soon be a Special Administrative Zone (SAR) of the People's Republic of China, and their friends, neighbours and relatives across the border, children and adults living only a short train journey away – where prostitution may result in the rapid spread of AIDS.

STREET CHILDREN

The use of children as part of the labour force remains common in many countries in Southeast Asia: on the land, in small factories, on plantations, in family businesses, as domestic help, on garbage sites, in tourism and in prostitution. There always have been – and probably always will be – children involved in family business as a way of contributing to the family economy. This is especially so in agricultural communities, and may be guarded against (for safety and health reasons) but never totally avoided or eradicated. Work of this nature is no doubt important for family cohesion, family stability and, if not excessive, the development of the individual.

As large numbers of families drift from the rural areas to towns and cities, the expectation that children will contribute continues; or, at least, that they will be self-sufficient in daily living. Street children are common in Thailand and the Philippines, and, to a lesser extent, in Malaysia. A 1990 issue of *Child Workers in Asia* suggested three categories of street children.

The first group are those who have families to which they return at the end of the day and are called 'children on the street'. They take to the street to supplement the family income before or after school. While they may spend the greater part of their working lives in the street, they continue to identify themselves with the communities where their families reside. Sometimes their street activities – begging, selling, stealing or even prostitution – are undertaken in conjunction with other members of the family. Not only street children but street families are among the fastest growing social phenomena in the poorest communities in Asia. One particular street family with which the author had considerable contact trundled a coffin-shaped cart along the streets. It contained the father's frail and almost lifeless body. Both cancer and tuberculosis were well advanced, his conditions untreated. Nevertheless, the man's wife struggled each evening to prepare clean school uniforms for the following day, an almost impossible task with no soap, little fresh water and nowhere to fold or store the children's garments. Within this first group, there are, of course, children who do not attend school at all, but what is common among them is the ties they endeavour to maintain with their respective families.

The second group, identified by the *Child Workers in Asia* report as 'children of the streets', are those who, for all practical purposes, live in the streets where they find shelter and sustenance. Their survival instinct forces them to establsh bonds with their peers who, one way or another, provide a support system. These children are exposed to the dangers of their environment almost the whole day that they are out in the street. While a number of them still have families, their ties are weak, and very rarely do most go home. The third group is made up of children who have been totally abandoned by their parents or guardians.

PROSTITUTION

Children in this third group, above, are, it would appear, those most likely to become involved with prostitution, making them the targets of paedophiles from both the East and the West. The majority of the paedophiles in Thailand and the Philippines are said to come from Australia, but Europeans are also common, notably Dutch, Swiss, German and British. Some centres for paedophiles have become internationally known, to paedophiles, through gay magazines in the West. *Spartacus* guide describes some towns in the Philippines as world holiday centres for paedophiles, ranking them above Sri Lanka where, for many years, boy prostitutes have plied their trade and been readily available. Significantly, German nationals can be charged in Germany with child sex offences committed in other countries. Meanwhile, changes in United Kingdom legislation are only just beginning to take place.

In late 1992, Britain's new criminal intelligence unit was called in to investigate the question of paedophilia involving Britons in countries such as the Philippines and Thailand. David Hamilton revealed in the *Sunday Express* on 8 November that the National Criminal Intelligence Service (NCIS) had in its possession a dossier containing the names of 40 child sex abusers, including 15 Britons. The dossier, compiled by Father Shay Cullen, an Irish Columban missionary priest who runs a refuge (called Preda) for street children in Olongapo, Philippines, had claimed that children as young as four years had been routinely abused in the Filipino sex industry. Certainly, the list of known cases in Asian countries continues to build, with child prostitution – as manifested in countries like Thailand and the Philippines – becoming a global problem.

Cullen has reported in other documents that sex freaks and paedophiles from all over the world have been attracted to Olongapo, a town that until the end of 1992 was the home of the US Seventh Fleet, based at Subic Bay. For more than ten years, while American servicemen were based in Olongapo, sexual activities with children were common, such incidents all too rarely resulting in charges or convictions. Servicemen were often moved to another station, ostensibly as part of a routine transfer, instead of being charged with sexual offences against children.

Cullen further asked in the *Sunday Express* article why the

Foreign Office and the Home Office had taken no action on known paedophiles who have abused Asian children. He stated: 'These abusers are intelligent, well-off businessmen – professional people such as doctors, lawyers and engineers. In many cases, they return to the UK with the most obscene holiday videos. The information I have handed to the police and other documents I am obtaining will give the police and the immigration people a legal basis to watch out for these people.'

One story by Cullen recounts the life of Chito who eventually found shelter at Preda:

Bright city lights mean nothing to Chito. He has little enough to celebrate as he hobbles barefoot along the street, weighed down by the two cans of water slung from a slender pole that is raising a raw welt on his skinny shoulder. Chito is a push-cart boy, the son of a trash collector who died two years previously, leaving three children and an emaciated wife, Lydia. She was working in a club. By 1992 she did not even have the strength to take in laundry for a living. Anna, the youngest sister, is just ten years old and helps her mother with the washing. Merly is six and gets little or no attention. She does not attend school. Chito has been taking care of the family since his father died.

Chito knows about life in jail. Frequently he has been there for a few days at a time for vagrancy, especially when the large US ships have been in port. He was made to clean out the faeces and urine in the toilet hole and had to sleep on the concrete floor listening to the scuffling and guffaws of men and women 'doing their thing' in the dark. If he was to eat he had to massage the criminal inmates until he was exhausted. One was dissatisfied and threw boiling water on him. he still has the scars.

He first met Trevor, his American friend, when he was eleven years of age. He went to the rented apartment near the American naval base with his mother to help with the laundry. Trevor gave him a candy bar, then ten pesos and later clothes, food and more money. It was a taste of paradise. He worshipped his blue-eyed God of Plenty. Trevor invited him into the apartment and showed him the wonders of a shower room and the magic of a television. Soon he was encouraged to try the shower and afterwards to sit on Trevor's lap watching television and sometimes falling asleep. One day he woke up in bed with his 'friend' beside him and it was not long before he was shown what games made Trevor happy and what made him angry. An angry scowl or a harsh word was sufficient to warn Chito that their games were secret. He quickly learned that it was the only way to keep the food and money flowing. His family depended on the gifts that Chito brought home and his mother and siblings never asked what he did that made Trevor so generous.

After an absence of several weeks from his 'friend', Chito came to want that food and money so much that his desire and need swamped his rising shame and revulsion of Trevor. So he went back. There was nobody in the compound but he could hear music from the apartment. 'Will he be angry with me for coming here after such a long absence?' the young boy wondered. He was nervous and frightened, but this passed as he stepped slowly into the living room and looked around at the polished furniture and gleaming television together with the bank of glowing stereo equipment shuttered behind two small glass doors. The memory of that first day in the house came back. He stood at the door and heard a soft crying. 'The child next door, perhaps,' he thought. He pushed the door and silently it opened. He saw Trevor in bed with Anna, his little sister. His mother was on the floor sleeping.

Chito, Anna and other children in similar circumstances make up the thousands of youngsters who are sexually abused or caught up in child prostitution in various countries in the region. As indicated above, both foreign tourists and local men are involved.

In an earlier book, *The Philippines: People, Poverty and Politics*, the present author gave an example of the ease with which it is possible to obtain a child for sexual activity, in this instance, in Olongapo city:

> The man on the corner of the street offers a 'woman'. The sailor refuses, but hesitates, and waits.
> 'Bit younger?' he enquires haltingly.
> The man replies, 'Cost more. Take a few mintues.'
> 'How much?'
> 'Fifty dollars for a virgin.'
> 'How old?'
> 'Twelve years.'
> The sailor nods.
> 'Wait here. Back in ten minutes.'
> The sailor waits. The man returns. Both move away down a side street, away from the bright lights. As in Manila, child prostitution thrives in Olongapo. Not only in Olongapo and Manila, but in Davao city and Bangkok.

AIDS

Coupled with prostitution in general and child prostitution in particular is the continuing threat of becoming HIV positive and contracting AIDS (Acquired Immunodeficiency Syndrome). While there are probably fewer reported cases of AIDS in Asia than in other parts of the world – for instance, in sub-Saharan Africa and parts of Latin America – the incidence is high in certain countries, for example, in parts of the Philippipines and Thailand. In a number of fishing villages in the west of Thailand, most women – and many children – in whole communities are known to have AIDS, the disease being spread through heterosexual contacts as a result of fishermen patronising prostitutes along the coast and returning to their home villages to infect their wives.

As reported by Renée Danziger in *Health Action* in November 1990, AIDS has serious and often painful implications for women in their role as actual or potential mothers. This has a particular significance, therefore, for teenage prostitutes, with evidence suggesting that between 25 and 40 per cent of infants born to HIV-infected mothers will be infected. Tragically, most children born with HIV infection will die before their fifth birthday. Looking after such children is particularly stressful for women who are themselves infected with HIV or who have AIDS. Young prostitutes in Manila, Bangkok and elsewhere in the region must, therefore, be regarded as being in the highest risk group as they move freely from client to client.

Of the 100 million street children in the world, the 1.2 million of them in the Philippines are representative of their Asian counterparts as they scavenge, beg, steal, sell cigarettes or offer sexual services. A report by the Agencies Welfare Fund in 1989 indicated that in Metro Manila – with a population of more than three million children and young people – there were as many as 75 000 street children. According to another report by the Philippine Mental Health Association in the same year, eight per cent of these children were engaged in prostitution.

During the opening of the first Regional Conference on Street Children in Asia in 1989, President Corazon Aquino admitted that, because of the lack of funds and resources, only 10 000 children were involved in social programmes.

At the same conference, Peter Tacon, executive director of Childhope, described how children in developing countries were often part of the international sex trade. Syndicates operating out of the United States, Australia, Japan, Germany and other European nations (as noted above) promoted 'sex tours' to impoverished countries, or lured children into pornography.

'People in industrialised countries thrive on the poverty in developing countries, and the most appalling part of it is that some of their citizens, especially the paedophiles ... take advantage of the situation by exploiting the children,' said Tacon.

A study presented during the 1989 conference – expressing sentiments equally valid in 1993 – showed that Filipino child prostitutes often suffer severe physical abuse at the hands of foreign clients, and are left with 'deep-seated psychological scars' which will affect them for the rest of their lives. This allegation was confirmed by other delegates from different countries in the region.

Although in their own country some children are exploited by Filipinos – relatives, family friends or foster parents – as has been shown in the case of Chito, foreign sex abusers known by the children as *Kano* (for Caucasians), *singkit ang mata* (for slitty-eyed) or *Hapon* (for Japanese) are of greatest concern.

Children use words which are a combination of English and Tagalog, and sometimes baby talk and onomatopoeic words to describe their experiences. Female child prostitutes are sometimes called *pa-cute*; male child prostitutes may be referred to as *koboys* (from 'cowboy' and 'call boy') and sexual intercourse is *dyug-dyug*, or 'enter'.

Reference has already been made to Olongapo city, until the end of 1992 the home of the US Seventh Fleet. The city's population of 3000 street children remains equally large in 1993. Behind the face of every child, as in Manila, crying 'one peso, sir' is a story of deprivation, degradation and despair. The children in Olongapo have well-defined areas of operation. The 'Victory Boys', for example, hang around the Victory line bus station, begging and, given the opportunity, picking pockets. Sometimes they move garbage for shopkeepers or storeholders, and occasionally go scavenging. There are no girls in this group.

The 'Magsaysay Kids', divided into sub-sections by their different locations, are those working nearest to the entrance of the former Subic Bay Naval Base. In addition to begging, the boys and girls working along Magsaysay Drive and Gordon Avenue 'watch' cars while the boys also scavenge. When the Americans were based at Subic Bay, begging could bring in a hundred pesos a day for children working along Magsaysay Drive; and with a recently arrived squadron of the Seventh Fleet in port, as much as five hundred pesos could be collected by one child during a single night. For very many – adults and children – the departure of the Americans was, it would appear, most significant in financial terms. To what extent it is replaced in the longer term by improved mental health and greater emotional stability will depend what it is possible to provide in terms of alternative resources, community facilities and a new level of sound concern.

Several 'fraternities' have been identified among the Magsaysay Kids. These include *Bahala na Gang* (the dominant group); *Sigue-Sigue Sputnik*; *Jacando*; and the *Alega Boys*.

There are no girls among the 'Solid Rag Pickers'. These boys collect junk around the city: bottles, plastic bags, cans and cardboard. The street pickings are piled on carts and hauled to junk shops in the most depressed areas of the city. The Solid Rag Pickers, apart from the child prostitutes, usually earn the most money.

There are no girls either among the 'Pushcart Boys'. These young lads hire a cart for an eight-hour period for 5 pesos and make about 30–50 pesos profit moving goods from the old market to the new market. The work is undertaken at night, from 1 a.m. to 6 a.m., with four o'clock the peak time.

The 'Plastic Kids' are the beginners. They hang around the vegetable and wet fish markets, buying four plastic bags for 1 peso, and selling each one for 50 centavos. The children then buy more bags, thereby earning 10–20 pesos a day.

As noted, there are 3000 street children in Olongapo city, aged from 5 to 14 years of age. The Pushcart Boys start when they are 13 and have sufficient strength to drag the carts. Members of the different fraternities know each other well and, in general, respect the territories of the others.

Reference has already been made in this chapter to child prostitutes. In Olongapo, they are drawn mainly from the Magsaysay Kids, who continue to beg when their pimps fail to find them clients. Some of the stall-holders at the entrance to the former Subic Naval Base are known to provide cover for well-organised syndicates offering sexual services from children. A significant number of children are introduced to this dollar-earning flesh trade as early as seven years of age. Besides injuries inflicted from both 'regular' and 'irregular' sex (namely, sado-masochism), the children's lack of sex education also makes them more prone to sexually transmitted diseases (STDs), with reference to the prevalence of AIDS having already been made earlier in the chapter. Many of the children regard STDs in much the same way as *sipon* (the common cold), a temporary but regular occurrence. The fear of AIDS, however, does bring to many a new sense of danger and urgency to avoid infection.

Angie was sometimes accompanied by her mother when the pimps took her to a client, or sometimes the mother and daughter went together to the hotel where the man was waiting. The mother told the director of the children's centre where Angie became a resident about her part in the sexual abuse of her daughter, and how she often waited outside the hotel to receive the 500 pesos paid by the customer for her daughter's services.

Angie's sexual exploitation continued for some time. In another three-generation family living together in a squatter community, the grandmother – who used to be a prostitute – acts as the contact point for her daughter and granddaughter, both prostitutes.

As in Thailand – and with similarly high social costs –

many Filipino children are used and abused at will. Some of the children who beg, or prostitute themselves, along Magsaysay Drive or Gordon Avenue in Olongapo city, and in areas of Manila, do not want to grow up. They earn more money as children and want to remain 'cute'. Some deliberately eat even less than their frail bodies need to consume, merely to remain small in stature and attractive to their clients.

As Olongapo street children become older, they move through the street hierarchy. Plastic Kids motivated to earn more money become Magsaysay Kids or – as they grow more muscular – Pushcart Boys. If they wish for an easier life, they may become one of the Victory Boys or, with a desire for their own 'business', may join the Solid Rag Pickers. However, some Pushcart Boys and Solid Rag Pickers would never join the Magsaysay Kids. They would be ashamed to beg.

Under the vagrancy laws, as in the case of Chito, street children in Olongapo are often picked up by the police. Although, under the law, they should not be held for more than six hours, often they are detained for longer, even for two or three weeks. The police expect the children to be bailed. The youngsters will frequently bail out their friends for 100–150 pesos. According to the children, when the police see that a child is unlikely to be bailed, they may make him a 'trustee' – put to work in the police compound for a week, cleaning and doing odd jobs. Most often the children are mixed with adult offenders, frequently hardened criminals.

In Olongapo, street children fall broadly into the three categories referred to earlier: those with regular contact with their families (about 70 per cent), those with irregular contact (about 20 per cent), and those who have been completely abandoned (about 10 per cent).

Some years ago, the Preda Human Development Centre in Olongapo, founded in 1973, as noted earlier, by a Roman Catholic priest, Father Shay Cullen, extended its original work with drug abusers to include some of the children in the city. The case example Chito was one of the boys among those who found a refuge at Preda.

Preda is just one of the many agencies – in Olongapo, in other parts of the Philippines and in Southeast Asia – providing a skeleton service for children in need. There is a soup kichen in Freedom Park and there are some residential homes in the city, but principally the workers serve as the street children's advocates, guides and friends.

There is a great flexibility of approach, and Preda has successfully developed its residential unit for street children, concentrating on two main groups: totally abandoned children and sexually exploited children. At the beginning of 1993, Cullen led a campaign to obtain compensation for American children left behind by US servicemen when the Seventh Fleet departed at the end of 1992.

Several of the children from Preda attend school on a regular basis. They long to be cared for, but by the age of ten many are compulsive beggars or have a heightened awareness of their sexual attractiveness and are easily drawn to the streets again.

Often Preda's new arrivals have to adjust to a different sleeping pattern. For most of their lives, they have worked by night, and slept by day.

As noted earlier, the pattern of deprivation, neglect and abuse is repeated in Manila, where not only street children but also street families are much in evidence. In order to survive – to keep alive from one day to the next – all members of the family may be involved in begging, pimping and prostitution.

Not far from the tourist area along Roxas Boulevard and in the heart of the 'red light' district between Malate Catholic Church and Malate Boys' School is the Halfway House (*Bahay Tuluyan*) catering for more than 200 children – mostly day care.

The problems appear even more severe than in Olongapo, with many of those coming to the centre being the children of prostitutes and street vendors. Consequently, they have to sleep at the centre while their parents work.

In addition to the car watchers, child prostitutes and scavengers, the staff of *Bahay Tuluyan* work with the 'solvent boys', drug dependent boys and the 'snatchers'. Snatching necklaces, watches, bags and cameras is now extremely common in Manila, as in many other major cities in the region.

Open twenty-four hours a day, *Bahay Tuluyan* caters for about 100 children in the four to seven age range, about 100 aged eight to 14 years; and 35 older adolescents.

There is very little structure in the centre, there are no conditions, and children are just free to participate. Because of the street experiences of the children, such an open nonjudgemental approach is the only one that has a hope of working.

Bahay Tuluyan is both a sad and exciting place – sad because of the rivers of pain flowing through the children's lives; exciting because of the alleviation of stress and distress, and the glimmers of hope that the centre brings to the few.

Where the children's parents exist – pimps, prostitutes, scavengers and street vendors – they are involved to the maximum extent possible. The parents are encouraged to offer support, particularly with legal and health concerns. Every other week a medical-dental clinic is held at the centre by the Makati Medical Society. The Remedios Circle Association pays for the medicines required by the young patients. Skin diseases, malnutrition and diarrhoea are the most common ailments.

There are other facets of the work, too, at *Bahay Tuluyan*. The older children – car watchers and drug dependents – have been made into a research team. They are encouraged to write down their experiences and to pass on information of concern to those involved with street children, thereby assisting in the documentation work of the centre.

For instance, it is now well known which 'flower sellers' in the district are those most easily willing and able to procure

Abuse, Neglect and Disease 41

child prostitutes. The territorial area of the pimps attaching themselves to the five-star hotels along Roxas Boulevard where child prostitution thrives is regarded as 'big business'.

A young boy or girl aged eight to 15 may receive 200 pesos for sexual services, while the pimp may receive as much as 4000 pesos for arranging the contact between the client and the child.

Drugs and glue sniffing too now have an increasing hold on the street children of Manila. 'Rugby', a glue used for shoe repairs is the current favourite, either sniffed by itself or mixed with a range of solvents, lacquer thinner or nail polish. Drug abuse among child prostitutes is now rampant, providing a temporary escape from the harsh realities of the children's existence.

For street children, the mixture of sexual exploitation and drug taking, or solvent abuse, pushes them towards a future underground world from which it will be difficult to escape.

The problem is now extensive, the resources limited. The answer is both political and economic. Certainly for the children it is economic. The last word in this section must be given to Sylvia, whose family is trapped in the spiral of poverty to which reference was made in Chapter 1. Sylvia is a 14-year-old prostitute, the daughter of a single parent, who has younger brothers and sisters. Encouraged by a social worker to move into a residential home and return to school Sylvia asked: 'Who will pay the rent? Where will the money come from except from my Japanese clients? Do you want us to become a street family?'

CHILDREN AND WAR

Throughout recent decades, the attention of the world has been drawn to the numerous conflicts that have occurred in the region: in Vietnam and Cambodia especially, in addition to the minor skirmishes elsewhere, and the constant stream of internal refugees in the Philippines. From Cambodia and

Vietnam came refugees in their thousands: over the border to Thailand from Cambodia and across the seas to Hong Kong from Vietnam. Some children remained with their families, some fell into the category of 'unaccompanied minors' and yet a third group comprised those who were born to mothers while they were refugees. In summary, these were all children of war, destined to be deprived to some extent of basic health care, education and nourishment. The stories associated with each child in this predicament are legendary: of neglect, abuse and hunger against a background of fear and terror together with levels of deceit and aggression necessary for mere survival. Some children and young people have found sanctuary, refuge and assistance in the huge refugee camps on the Thai-Cambodian border and in the refugee camps and detention centres in Hong Kong but, overall, the treatment of the children has amounted to neglect by a global system which permits so many millions of youngsters to live through their formative years with little or no education and inadequate food in conditions of squalor; neglect of an order which adds up to systematic and multi-faceted abuse.

In the Philippines many children have been at risk as internal refugees for more than twenty years, with hundreds being injured or losing their lives when literally caught in the crossfire of the New People's Army (NPA) and the government forces: witnessing summary executions, seeing their parents tortured or killed, being themselves shot or physically attacked, or used as human shields, or becoming messengers or young soldiers on one side or the other – no aspect of childhood was preserved. These, indeed, became children without childhood.

For some years, there have been organisations, operating initially from Manila, that have been endeavouring to assist children caught up in the internal warfare in the Philippines. These non-govermental organisations (NGOs) aim to help children of war 'to become children again'.

The Children's Rehabilitation Centre (CRC) chapter on

Panay Island, in Western Visayas, attends to children's education together with their medical and nutritional needs, but its major programme continues to be psycho-social rehabilitation. The debilitating effects of war on children are undoubtedly psychological. Having experienced kilings, evacuations, hostage-taking, starvation, arrests and detention, they are the extremely vulnerable victims of armed conflict. In 1992, the CRC on Panay had 43 children in its care but with an increase every month following an escalation of armed conflict on the island. Considered the country's 'rice bowl', Panay has been the site of some of the fiercest battles between the Armed Forces of the Philippines (AFP) and the NPA.

CRC, the only NGO of its kind on the island, serves children who are either the direct or indirect victims of armed activities initiated by the NPA or the AFP. Among the youngest beneficiaries of its services in 1992 was a two year old whose father was killed in 1990 by the paramilitary Citizen Armed Force Geographical Unit in an evacuation centre in Antique province, 425 kilometres southeast of Manila. The oldest beneficiary during the same year was a 17-year-old boy whose father was killed in an NPA ambush. Children accommodated in the CRC display a range of recurring problems, the most common behavioural dysfunctions including nightmares, nervousness in the presence of people in uniforms, and panic at the sight of guns, blood and helicopters. They tend to withdraw from people, exhibit disruptive habits in games, show little interest in studies, and have difficulty in following instructions. Many of these characteristics are similar to those shown by children confined to the detention centres in Hong Kong. Although different in source, nature and intensity, the Vietnamese children in Hong Kong are also victims of war.

One further group, more immediately and directly seen as victims of war, are those children who have lost their limbs or their lives as they walk across the fields of their native lands, namely in Laos, Vietnam and Cambodia, and trigger off unexploded devices buried near the surface of the soil.

These devices are the legacy of occupying armies which have failed, accidentally or deliberately, to clear their minefields prior to departure. The resulting injuries to children remain horrific, and it is not uncommon to find whole communities where children are forced to rely on artificial limbs, the gift of organisations like the Cambodia Trust based in Oxford, UK.

CHILDREN IN AFFLUENT SOCIETIES

The horror in the lives of the children already discussed in this chapter is not immediately mirrored in the lives of children growing up in the richer countries, for instance Hong Kong, Singapore, South Korea and Taiwan, although they, too, have aspects of their existence which reflect adversely on the individual countries and on the standards of care given to children world-wide. Both groups – that is, those in the poorest, developing nations whose parents do not care for them, and those living in more affluent societies – have children whose parents neglect and abuse them, inflict physical and emotional punishment, deprive them of affection, sometimes abuse them sexually and, despite sufficient financial means, fail to provide a familial and educational milieu in which children can grow and flourish to their maximum potential.

Children in affluent societies also have their own, very different problems. As parental incomes rise, so children themselves have greater spending power, becoming easily caught up in the unending pull of consumerism, and the way it draws young people to experiment with what they perceive as 'attractive' patterns of behaviour, for example, smoking, drinking and drug abuse; all of which (together with the increased consumption of 'junk food') affect their physical and mental health. The result is children and young people who are inadequately equipped for parenthood at a later stage of their lives, and who have a lack of interest in making a contribution to the lives of their family members or to the communities – and wider society – in which they live. In too many instances, they also reject the educational opportunities made available to them by the countries in which they live, opportunities which many of those in the least developed countries strive for in vain because of corrupt or weak administrations, low family incomes or poorly qualified teachers and instructors.

Looked at objectively, such problems cannot be regarded as comparable and must be considered – as in the case of child prostitution and children caught up in war in the poorer nations – country by country and problem by problem.

CHILD SUICIDES

The figures relating to student suicides in South Korea in 1989 alarmed both educationalists and parents alike. A report from the Ministry of Education showed that there was a suicide every three days in the country's elementary and high schools. At that time, Japan too appeared to be suffering from an alarming increase in such tragedies. While recognised as a frightening phenomenon of affluent societies – variously blamed on the lack of parental involvement in their children's lives, school 'pressures', the media, and the inadequacy of governments in providing appropriate pupil–school social worker ratios – the years from 1990 onwards were especially horrific in Hong Kong, where the numbers of pupils choosing to take their own lives rose dramatically to the point where the issue was highlighted, and rightly so, as one in which the efforts of the whole society – parents, teachers, pupils, social workers and legislators – had to combine to reverse this lemming-like flight towards self-destruction, which had become the solution for so many children and young people. Hong Kong has only one educational psychologist for every 40 000 pupils compared with one per 5000 in the United Kingdom.

Figures released by the Hong Kong Education Department

on 8 January 1993 showed a significant increase in suicides and attempted suicides during the previous two years:

September 1992 to January 1993: 14 suicides and 30 attempts
1991–2 school year: 21 suicides and 46 attempts
1990–1 school year: 3 suicides and 32 attempts
1989–90 school year: 1 suicide and 25 attempts
1988–9 school year: 2 suicides and 23 attempts

On 9 January 1993, the suicide of a 12-year-old girl, who plunged to her death from her Wong Tai Sin home, brought the number of child suicides to three in one week. The girl's death occurred just two hours before an 11-year-old boy was twice prevented from committing suicide: first by police who grabbed him when he tried to jump from his home; then by rescue workers when he was persuaded to come down from a precarious perch on his school building. The boy's headmaster believed that the boy was extremely upset by his parents recent separation, and was trying to attract attention. The headmaster said that, additionally, the boy had complained about having to prepare meals and look after his younger sister. From the headmaster's point of view, the boy had also misbehaved at school, playing truant, and biting and kicking classmates and teachers, much of which had been linked to his unhappiness over his parents separation.

On 9 January 1993, the editorial in the *Hong Kong Standard* analysed the problem:

As Hong Kong residents, we are shocked and horrified by the nightmare plagues of student suicides that have cursed the past two academic years. As parents, many of us worry about the emotional pressures suffered by our own children.

Why have so many of our young people chosen to take that tragic way out? What is wrong with our society that these children who are 'dead by their own decision' have said in effect: 'If this is humanity, I want no more of it.'

We definitely need more school social workers but that is not the whole answer . . . The schools have come in for a certain amount of blame. Some parents have cited an education system that burdens students with extensive homework, frequent examinations and pressure to excel.

Teachers say the parents themselves are demanding that their children be given more work. They are not satisfied if they do not see red marker lines in the homework books and if their offspring are not given tests every two weeks or so.

Part of the problem is the fact that the traditional Chinese family, which was very much an extended family network, has broken down.

Today's nuclear family unit, in which both parents may be working, often fails to provide children with an outlet for their anxieties or an opportunity to express their feelings. Auntie is no longer there. Nor is Granny. And many young people may feel that they have to keep their emotions hidden.

By contrast, a survey in Singapore has found that the majority of young people canvassed believe that they have been blessed with stable homes and consider the family the most important thing in life. Significantly, the student suicide rate there is very low.

A residential nursery: clean and clinical. However, with no toys, the children are unstimulated. With few adults to talk to them, language development is frequently impaired.

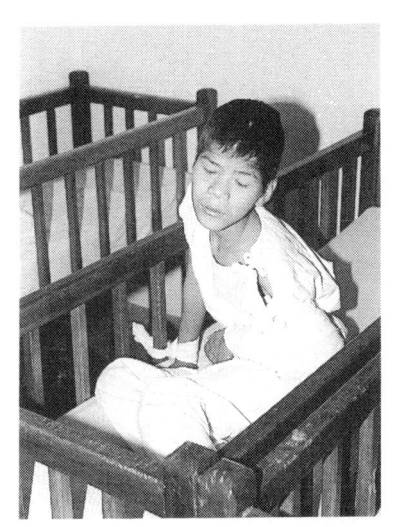

Handicapped children are too often tied to their beds.

These children live in a leper colony for Christians and Muslims.

This girl is the lead singer in the school band. Blindness among children is prevalent throughout the region.

Learning braille in Brunei.

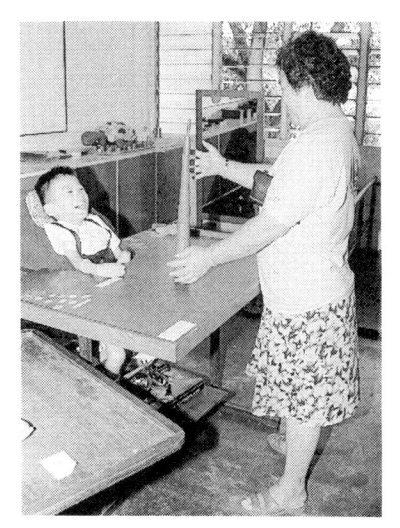

In Malaysia, there is increased parental participation in children's learning, particularly in cases where children have special needs.

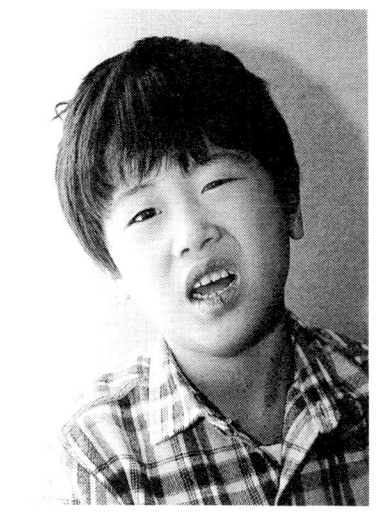

This Korean boy is autistic but is responding slowly to stimulation.

Early education in Thailand remains comparatively formal.

Recent influence in Lao PDR has resulted in the widespread acceptance of new ideas.

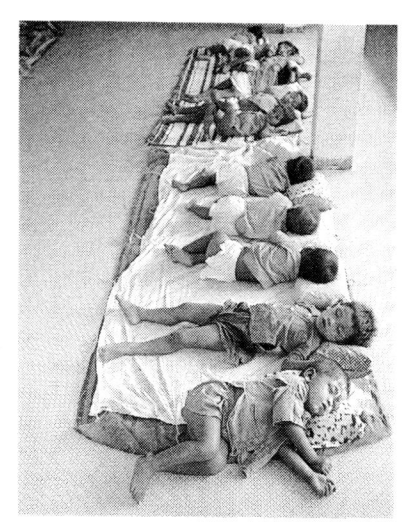

An early afternoon siesta for young children is common practice in Asia.

The author with two young girls who attend a day centre in Bangkok. (Photo: Anon.)

Young boys are often involved in commercial enterprises.

Children are extensively employed in the fishing industry in Thailand.

Feeding the hungry millions in Asia is an never-ending task. This picture was taken in a children's home in Thailand.

These children from a rich family are attending a wedding in Manila Cathedral.

A Buddhist family in Thailand at their evening devotions.

A youth worker in Manila counsels young drug addicts.

CHILDREN WITHOUT CHILDHOOD

There are indeed throughout Asia many thousands of children without childhood.

Street families are an increasingly visible feature of Asian countries.

Eventually, the spirit of youth will carry the region forward.

4
CONCERN AND INTERVENTION

As suggested at the beginning of Chapter 3, the outlook for many children living in Southeast Asian countries is gloomy. This is especially so in developing countries where, despite aid from other parts of the world, poverty, sickness, disease and exploitation continue to ravage the underprivileged millions, making it foreseeably impossible for the citizens of many countries – in terms of high population growth, income levels, housing, job opportunities and the quest for an improved quality of life – to have any immediate hope of equating their lifestyles with those of their richer neighbours in, for instance, Hong Kong, Japan, Singapore, South Korea and Taiwan. The contrasts between the rich and the poor in Southeast Asia are probably more noticeable than in any other part of the world. The effects are felt particularly by the children who move into the next generation with no better prospects for their own children, most strikingly in respect of education, health care and exploitation. Statutory social services, where they exist (minimally in Thailand, the Philippines, South Korea and Malaysia), generally remain under-developed; the needs and the rights of children have scarcely been articulated on a country-by-country basis; and, in countries where children survive, rather than thrive, they often do so simply by means of age-old and sometimes worn-out traditional child-rearing practices which give little hope for an overall forward movement – either regionally or in individual countries – in the necessary, indeed vital, surge towards a new understanding of child care, child protection, child development and children's rights.

In those countries claiming to have a higher level of societal development, there is a quite different set of lifestyles – sometimes involving exaggerated consumerism, drug abuse, a high consumption of cigarettes and alcohol, excessive educational stress, parental neglect, poor safety records and codes of conduct, and tense adult–child relationships; there is often insufficient parental education to ensure that children are provided throughout their formative years with the nurturing, protection, values education (for instance, towards the environment), and the emotional and social climate essential for their movement towards young adulthood.

GLIMMERS OF HOPE

The contents of this book have presented a dismal picture of the lives of many children in Southeast Asia. The sadness of this picture must not be minimised, as for most youngsters it is an accurate portrayal of life as it is, and will continue to be for some time, probably well into the 21st century.

Everywhere, however, it is possible to find examples of good practice where dedicated staff – frequently with inadequate resources – struggle to provide a service which contributes immeasurably to the quality of life of children who are otherwise destined for inhumanity, cruelty, abuse, exploitation, sickness, emotional rejection, physical isolation and even premature death. It seems to be most important to remain constantly alert to these evils and injustices, to be responsive to them as far as this is possible, to devise programmes and policies which contribute to overall change, but not to be devastated by the distortions in the upbringing of children and child care practices with which the author has been so frequently faced in making this social inventory of child care in Southeast Asian countries.

Many examples of high quality work have been found, and

some of these have already been referred to earlier in the text, notably the work undertaken in the House of Friendship in Mindanao, Philippines (Chapter 1), and with street children in the same country – by Preda in Olongapo city and by *Bahay Tuluyan* in Manila (Chapter 3).

One aspect of work with children that finds universal support almost throughout the region – by government and non-government organisations alike – is the care of pre-school children. This is found, of course, as would be expected, in the richer territories, namely Hong Kong and Singapore, but also, with equal concern if not equal efficiency and resources, in Thailand, Malaysia, South Korea and surprisingly, given the poverty in the country, in the People's Democratic Republic of Laos (Lao PDR), this last as a result of close cooperation between Valerie Emblen (a lecturer at the University of North London and a staff member of Save the Children Fund) and Daovong Vongsay, the Deputy Director of the Teacher Training Department in the Ministry of Education, in Vientiane, Lao PDR.

One of the most important models for the care, protection, development and education (in the widest sense) of pre-school children must be the unit attached to the Regional Training and Resource Centre in Early Childhood Care and Education for Asia (National Trade Unions Congress) based in Singapore. The Centre itself has six objectives:

- to highlight innovative ways of working with children and families
- to disseminate information on the findings of projects
- to provide an update on trends and development in the area of early childhood, particularly in the region
- to provide information on different types of resources available in this field
- to exchange information and experiences
- to publicise relevant conferences, forums and other related events

With superb facilities and first-class equipment, the Centre staff work purposively and competently with the young children in their charge, providing a service to parents and the community to which workers in some other countries can only aspire. Not so, however, in parts of Thailand and Malaysia where funding for the provision for pre-school children is very different. Nevertheless, in these two countries, work with pre-school children is also approached most seriously in terms of facilities, the professionalism of the staff and the relaxed atmosphere in which the infants 'work' purposefully each day on their journey towards the commencement of their more formal educational programme at the infant and junior school stage. One of the most important initiatives with this youngest group of children is, as noted, taking place in Lao PDR, where an advanced kindergarten system, catering for children from three or four months up to the age of six, when the youngsters go to primary school, is showing dividends which, a few years ago, would have been considered impossible. On her return to the UK from Lao, Emblen, in association with her former colleague Vongsay, wrote about developments in the country:

> ... the purpose of this article is not to create a negative view of the situation ... It is a time of development and there are a number of enthusiastic and knowledgeable educationalists, in kindergartens and in the Ministry of Education, who are developing a more child-centred approach to the care of young children. Attempts to encourage more play are hampered by lack of materials. Nothing is wasted; everything is used. I was watching a video which was intended to show teachers how to make low cost toys. The programme showed a doll's house made from a cardboard box. The teacher who sat next to me said, 'If I had a box like that I would use it as a cupboard.' The education system will not be able to supply even basic materials such as paper or pencils in the foreseeable future. The challenge is to

create a more active, problem-solving approach which does not need a lot of materials. Local educationalists are making very creative moves in this area and are examining the resources they have. The Lao culture is linguistically very rich, especially in songs and stories. The story-telling tradition was interrupted soon after the Liberation by the suppression of a number of traditional tales and their replacement by consciously moral stories: Aesop's fables are used a great deal, possibly deriving from the French curriculum in colonial days.

Writing in *Toward a Fair Start for Children*, part of the 'Young Child and the Family Project 1990–95', Robert Myers stated:

> The cognitive development of infants living in environments with little variety is generally lower than that of infants living in environments that contain variety. The implication is that attention should be given to determining the degree of variety present in different environments and to either reinforcing or adding to that variety, according to the needs of the particular child. (Most environments offer variation and there is no need to import things or people to provide needed variation ...) [The] social experience of a child will usually have a much stronger influence on future achievement, IQ score, and socially deviant behaviour than condition at birth. In short, a benevolent environment is critical. It is possible for recuperation to occur in such an environment, even in relatively high 'at risk' circumstances related to conditions at birth.

In respect of the arguments put forward for investing in early childhood development programmes, Myers divides the world into believers and sceptics, the former underlining the importance of good care and attention for children during their earliest months and years, the latter showing a lack of understanding, taking refuge in financial considerations or – having themselves grown up in advantaged conditions, in a loving home, with food on the table and good health care, and with parents who provided a stimulating environment for growing and learning – feeling that families can and do automatically provide the attention needed for healthy growth and development.

Myers further states that the 1959 Declaration of Children's Rights and the 1989 Convention on the Rights of the Child suggest that the right for children to develop to their full potential is widely accepted internationally, providing the cornerstone for an early childhood programme rationale. Certainly, some of the work being undertaken in certain Southeast Asian countries – both rich and poor – bears witness to this, and gives hope to the youngsters whose period of infancy will straddle the years around the turn of the century. As Myers concludes:

> ... the rhetoric of human rights needs to be translated into action. Children are not able to make that translation for themselves. They are dependent on the actions of others for their rights.

The time spent by the author in Lao PDR, and especially in the Pre-school Teacher Training School at Dongdok and in other kindergartens in the region, is among the highlights of his research endeavour in the field of the care and education of Southeast Asian children. It is gratifying to experience the high levels of concern and positive action focused on the needs of very young children, a strategy which is both rewarding and far-reaching in its impact on the overall practice area and policy development in the region.

Unfortunately, the same cannot be said of many of the residential facilities for young children which too often accentuate the institutional nature of any 'home' away from a child's own home, with rows of tiny cots supposedly catering for the needs of this younger age group.

Indeed, the institutionalisation process is manifested throughout residential provision in both the developed and under-developed countries in the region. Japan, Singapore and Hong Kong have residential homes and schools for very large groups of children, with parents often preferring the 'neutrality' and somewhat impersonal nature of large units to any option of foster care. The idea of other adults, in an intimate quasi-parental role, caring for their children becomes too much of a threat to the natural parents, who will accept only 'institutional care' or a complete return home. No alternative can be considered.

That many residential units are often too large, there is no doubt. Seoul, with its Boystown, and Manila with its Boystown and adjacent Girlstown, are examples of the way not to proceed, despite the levels of care which the young sisters appear to give to their charges. All current knowledge points to the damaging effects on children of living in complexes for 3000 young people, even when broken down into units of 300 and with staff members making every effort to personalise the care that is given.

The work undertaken at Preda and by the House of Friendship and *Bahay Tuluyan* in the Philippines has provided examples of current attempts to make inroads into outdated approaches to the care of children in groups. There are also other important models of care, both in the Philippines and in other countries in the region to which reference should be made.

The Asian Social Institute was founded in Manila in 1962 by the late Very Revd Dr Francis Senden, a Dutch missionary. A philosopher and sociologist, he sought to train socially-oriented leaders among Filipinos and other Asians. Through a study of the social sciences he hoped that leaders would utilise social and research skills for the improvement of social, economic and political conditions. The Senden Home for Boys is a project of the Institute. Although the boys live in a comparatively modern building about an hour's drive from the centre of Manila (two and a half hours by public transport), by western standards the home is sparse in furniture and equipment. There is no cutlery, and there is no point in replacing the original supply. Most items have quietly disappeared, to be sold on the streets. In company with other Asians, very many Filipinos eat with their fingers, anyway.

The Senden Home can only be viewed within the context and culture of a country where the mass of the people live in poverty. Undoubtedly, there is a feeling of calm and cooperation at the home. This is not, of course, to say that there are not problems in working with 24 boys with an age range of approximately seven to 18 years, but the background of the home and of the boys makes these difficulties rather special.

Although subject to a few general conditions of the central government, Senden Home is free to admit and discharge boys at will. Some stay for many years, and there is a family atmosphere. Homeless, or physically and sexually abused, or thrown out by their families, or orphaned, they have wandered the streets of Manila, falling into the hands of gangs who have led them into delinquency or begging, the latter a highly syndicated activity. When begging is not simply a family affair, one adult will have had four or five youngsters working for him, and he in turn will have been managed by somebody else, and expected to turn in a regular supply of money and goods. According to the boys, while 'working the streets', transgression of the gang rules will have meant punishment by the older members. In addition to violent beatings, some of the boys may have been made to perform the most bizarre sexual acts in front of other boys, to heighten their sense of shame.

It is from these conditions that boys will have arrived at Senden Home. Sometimes a resident will return to the home after a day or two in Manila with another boy he has rescued from the streets. He may go back with three or four others, especially if the boys are young and only on the threshold of delinquency.

Boys do run off. After a few days' rest and regular meals the call of the city is sometimes strong, in many ways parallel to the feelings experienced by the residents of Preda in Olongapo city. The majority of the boys return voluntarily. They may need to go and return several times before accepting Senden as their home. The boys themselves decide when they want to leave, and they are often much older than 18 years.

Senden has a totally non-punitive regime, and the boys go to local schools. They keep ducks and rear pigs, some of which are huge. The visit by the author included one day when 24 university students (from privileged backgrounds) had organised a medical mission, bringing along a group of doctors and dentists. Two boys had serious dental problems, one with a double set of front teeth.

Many aspects of the Senden Home make it of particular interest. There is an absence of the close supervision associated with most residential homes for boys. Problems that do arise are worked out by the group as a whole, and this is an important part of the Senden philosophy. Six boys are members of the home council. Bedtime is 9 p.m. and the boys are up and about by 5.30 a.m. Again, as in many Asian countries, the concept of 'shame' is one of the strongest cultural traits: many boys feel their poverty acutely, and nothing is worse than being scolded in public. As adults, people have been known to kill rather than 'lose face'.

One and a half hours flying time from the Philippines, in Hong Kong, the Hong Kong Student Aid Society provides a range of homes for children and young people, all purposeful, dynamic establishments offering a high standard of care and education. One of the larger homes is being extended in line with modern developments in child care, and will have a number of smaller group homes attached, with the main unit used by the satellites for training, supervision and support. The Hong Kong Student Aid Society remains in the forefront of subvented non-government organisations in the territory, offering models of child care in the run-up to 1997 when Hong Kong becomes a Special Administrative Region of the People's Republic of China (PRC). Residential care in the PRC still appears to be very much a 'junior prison' model, unaffected by what is appropriate for the developmental needs of the child.

The beginning of the Hong Kong Student Aid Society can be traced to 1957, when two orphan boys in Rennies Mill were given food and accommodation by the founder, D.G.M. Taylor, who was later assisted by a small committee of missionaries and others who worked together on behalf of the orphans. The Mark Memorial Home was fully operational by 1960 when it was officially opened.

In 1965, in response to a growing demand for places, Island Hostel on Lantau Island, the second residential unit, was opened together with Tung Wan Primary School, designed for 'late starters'. The hostel was located in some derelict bungalows vacated by the company which had built the nearby Shek Pik Reservoir. The Island Hostel caters for 60 boys.

Two years later, in 1967, Holland Hostel was built at Kwun Tong, Kowloon, Hong Kong, with funds provided by the Dutch Reformed Churches of the Netherlands. With 110 places for adolescent boys, the residents of Holland Hostel study in various secondary schools in the urban area.

The high quality of the everyday work and the dedication of the staff are further highlighted by a tragic incident which took place in one of the Hong Kong Student Aid Society's establishments in 1985. On 19 July in that year, Liu Ip-wan Philip, 25 years of age, a residential social worker from the Island Hostel, and 11-year-old Chan Kwok-choi, a resident of the hostel, were drowned trying to rescue a boy who had fallen into a water-catchment in the Lantau Island (South) Country Park, Lantau being one of the many islands offshore from Hong Kong in the South China Sea.

Soon after Liu Ip-wan and the 16 boys he was accompanying arrived at the park, it began to rain and the current became stronger. Despite a warning not to go near the catchment, one of the group climbed down to the water's edge, at first putting one foot into the water then slipping and falling in completely. Liu Ip-wan and the other boys immediately ran to the catchment and stretched out their hands, trying to reach the victim. During this attempt Chan Kwok-choi also slipped and fell into the water. Both were soon swept away by the strong current. Eventually the boy who had first fallen into the water managed to grab the sidewall and climbed to safety. Liu Ip-wan ran alongside the catchment towards the direction of the Shek Pik Reservoir and, on reaching Chan Kwok-choi, jumped into the water and held him in his arms.

Liu Ip-wan remained calm throughout the accident. From the time that he saw what was happening until he jumped into the water only a couple of minutes elapsed. During that brief period he instructed the boys to report to the police, intentionally put down his keys on the bank and ran alongside the catchment. He would have known that the place where he jumped was very near the end of the catchment, and that unless he took action at that moment his young companion would have no chance of being rescued. Liu Ip-wan stood in the catchment holding the boy in his arms and struggled for about 15 seconds before both disappeared beneath the swirling water. The worker might have been able to save his own life had he been prepared to give up his hold on the boy.

Apart from residential nurseries and the very large residential homes and schools already referred to (in Manila, Tokyo, Seoul and elsewhere), an interesting range of work is being undertaken in smaller units in other parts of the region. One of the most unusual, unexpected and exciting residential establishments was 'discovered' near Kanchanaburi in Thailand, adjacent to the River Kwai and about 50 kilometres north of the famous bridge. Here, grouped around a community hall in what amounted to a clearing in the forest, was a group of eight or ten structures made of locally available materials (trees and reeds). Each residence was the home of about 20 children and young people, all of whom were being given a 'liberal' education based on the model and philosophy of A.S. Neill, the well-known author of *Summerhill*, whose pioneer work in the UK contributed considerably to the foundation of a more *laissez-faire* approach to the care and education of children experiencing emotional and educational difficulties. The principal of the community had spent time in the UK – at Summerhill – and was endeavouring with considerable success to implement the model in an eastern setting. The children were relaxed, the community meetings were purposeful and participatory, and the residential units provided a stimulating environment in which the young people could develop. In the 'house' in which the author stayed, the young residents were among the friendliest group of children and young people to be found in any part of the world, showing an eagerness to communicate and exchange ideas often surpassing the enthusiasm of their counterparts in Europe, and reflecting the ability and willingness of Asian youngsters to participate whenever they are given the opportunity.

Equally stimulating but more controlled are the establishments run by the Ministry of Community Development in Singapore: the two boys' homes, and the girls' home, all displaying work by both staff and residents of a very high order. An important unit was also found in Kuala Lumpur in Malaysia, where adolescent girls, mostly Muslims, were being assessed with a view to a return home or to being found an alternative long-term placement. For a supposedly controlled and controlling environment, the atmosphere of the home was most relaxed with, for example, a particular involvement by the girls – as in Singapore – in catering, and the provision of well-presented, attractive, nourishing dishes.

With exceptions, the provision – particularly residential provision – made for children with special needs (namely, those experiencing visual and auditory impairment, and others who have various mental and physical handicaps) is far from reaching the goals aspired to in the various UN declarations of the rights of the child. However, some individual projects are staffed by personnel and have equipment and facilities which would only be expected in countries with the highest income levels and the best-trained staff. In Indonesia, South Korea, Laos and Brunei, the last especially, it is possible to find extremely effective work being undertaken under even the poorest conditions and with limited budgets, given the goodwill of staff and an adequate supply of day-to-day equipment for basic learning and care. This is sad, considering the almost inexhaustible supply of riches of the Sultan of Brunei. Most often in the richer countries, improving the quality of child care provision is a question of income redistribution, whereas in the poorest and least developed countries what appears to count most is local concern, local enthusiasm and the transmission of a small number of skills and policies by overseas advisers and specialists (as manifested by the work of Valerie Emblen in Lao PDR), who are able to grasp problems quickly, make a swift analysis and provide a method of organising and proceeding which brings about sufficient change to enable the local community to continue to manage its own affairs.

Korea

Apart from criticism about the size of its over-large residential units, little has been said in this text about one particular country, South Korea, a country described by the author in an earlier article as 'the flipside of a miracle'.

In a land of physically healthy and well-dressed children, Korean youngsters are, in some ways, already paying the price of growing up as citizens of one of the 'economic miracles' of Asia. Although, compared with countries like Thailand, the Philippines and even Indonesia, there is relative rather than absolute poverty, the gap between rich and poor continues to widen.

Welfare provision, which fails to keep pace with needs and expectations, is developing only slowly against a background of political intrigue and tradition.

Politically, those in the South have an increasing compulsion towards reunification with the people in the Communist North. Practically, in 1993, however, despite slow changes, there appears no immediate answer to how reunification may be brought about. North and South Korea are one in culture, tradition and language, and should be reunited.

The country was divided into two at the end of the Second World War. Not a great deal is known about child welfare in North Korea. However, there is an extensive network of nursery school provision, and the education system has been rigorously developed. As in the South, defence costs have for many years been high in North Korea, and this has drained away money that could have been used for welfare projects. Psychiatric services remain under-developed, there is no school social work service, no educational psychologists (in 1990), fostering is largely unknown, and there is an over-reliance on residential care, especially in the huge units referred to earlier.

Unlike many other Asian countries, there seem to be no widespread problems of child labour in South Korea, although incidents of individual abuse occur in both rural and urban areas. As elsewhere, migration to the cities cannot be stemmed and – in a country of 43 million people – the population of the capital, Seoul, approaches 11 million.

More than 95 per cent of children of school age attend high school, although post-primary education is not compulsory. In South Korea, there is a literacy rate of 98 per cent.

As in Hong Kong, Singapore and Japan, school pressures are among the major difficulties facing children and parents. Any sacrifice will be made by South Korean parents to have the distinction of a child admitted to one of the nations's elite universities, a feature of the society comparable to the enthusiasm and determination of parents in Japan. Many parents arrange special tuition for childen attending infant schools, with a view to improving their chances at primary and secondary levels, and of university entrance at a later date. The suicide figures among children and adolescents in South Korea for the year 1989 have already been noted in Chapter 3, one more testimony to young people's reactions to excessive school pressures.

Professor Kwang-iel Kim has reported on child abuse in Korea. In a paper to a world congress in Athens in 1989, he stated: 'Clinical and social interest in family violence has a rather short history in Korea. But there is no statement of any system for prevention and professional help in the law.'

In 1979, the Korean Society for Social Welfare opened the Child Abuse Centre in Seoul, but closed it one year later because cases were not being reported. In 1983, a 'Children's Hotline' began to operate in Seoul (run by the Korea Crusade), becoming active through professional advice and social investigation. As elsewhere in the region – and the world – the reported rate of child abuse is much influenced by definition, criteria and the methodology of any survey. Shin (1986) reported that in South Korea 98 per cent of 360 children in the age group range 11 to 15 years were 'battered' at least once by their parents over a period of one year. The Korean Children's Crusade (1987) surveyed 1245 11 and 12 year olds and reported that more than 97 per cent had been battered at least once during their lifetime by a family member or a non-family member, 46 per cent were battered at least once a month, and 18 per cent at least once a week. Compared with American findings, child battering in South Korea is high. According to the Korean Survey Gallup Polls (1980), 72 per cent of Korean mothers often administer physical punishment to their children, whereas in Japan the figure is 33 per cent, in the United States 26 per cent, in Thailand 23 per cent, and in the UK 28 per cent.

Rapid industrialisation and urbanisation in South Korea during the last two or three decades – with the resultant family disorganisation – have brought about the 'child-headed family'. This is defined as a family of children under 18 years of age living together without parents or responsible adults.

At the end of the 1980s, there were 15 000 children in nearly 7000 child-headed families in Korea. Many of the family heads were under 12 years of age, the children existing in unstable living conditions by means of government subsidies for rice, barley, heating and school fees.

These government programmes are complemented by the Korea Children's Foundation (KCF) through local sponsorship programmes on a national scale. The KCF is the largest voluntary child care organisation in Korea. The Foundation also manages, on behalf of the Ministry of Health and Social Affairs, a Child Finding Centre (CFC). The number of missing children has been increasing year by year, and is now a major social issue. They are classified either as 'pure' or as 'suspicious' missing children, basically those who have been abandoned or those who have been kidnapped by unknown persons. About 4000 children go missing each year. Of these, 900 will be placed in residential centres when they are found.

Among other positive child care initiatives being undertaken by the KCF are services for handicapped children, the establishment of children's day care centres and some residential homes. The emphasis of the KCF is on maintaining children in the community whenever possible, at a time when the government has committed itself to the development of nearly 250 day care centres by the end of 1994.

The KCF is actively seeking to develop further its fostering programme, a difficult task in that particular country. In Korea, family blood ties are highly valued and traditionally – as in several other Asian countries – Korean people have preferred sons to daughters. Consequently, throughout the early 1990s, fostering has been virtually unknown, while placement for overseas adoption has remained quite common.

This is expected to end in 1996 when the government intends to cancel its previously extensive overseas adoption programme. Intensive new developments will be required in respect of domestic adoption and fostering.

Domestic adopters in Korea have always imposed stringent conditions: they want children of the same blood type, adopter-like appearance, good health and high intelligence, a matching process that goes some way to explain why there remains an excessive demand for residential places for children, particularly for those with mental and physical handicap.

The Village of Greater Love, an impressive facility for profoundly handicapped children from one to 16 years has been developed as one of the KCF projects, catering for 100 children. A full range of rehabilitation and treatment is provided, together with special education for those able to benefit from it. Seventy per cent of the children are totally dependent, about the same percentage have been abandoned, and only one boy appeared able to stand upright without assistance. Most of the children are incontinent.

A feature of the home is the large number of volunteers, about 500 per month, and the professional service includes an Individualised Programme Plan. Here, indeed, at the Village of Greater Love, was found a caring, professional group of staff, working in a positive environment with the most disadvantaged children in the country.

Children of mixed race

One phenomenon not yet discussed but which remains an important issue, is the increase in the region in the number of children of mixed race. These children may be divided into three groups: (i) those who are the often unwanted children of prostitutes, the offspring of rape victims, perhaps as the result of armed conflict, or the neglected and abandoned children of members of the armed forces of a particular country serving overseas; (ii) those whose parents are both of Asian origin but from different countries; and (iii) those of truly mixed marriages where, frequently, one parent (usually the father) is Caucasian and the other Asian.

Not all children of mixed race face problems during their formative years. Many move through childhood and adolescence with growing confidence and a firm sense of personal identity, especially in cases where they are helped to develop increasing pride in their two family nationalities, occasionally to speak two languages and to have a sense of two cultural traditions. Many of the offspring of mixed marriages are particularly attractive children with natural abilities to communicate, to relate and to excel. Mixed marriages between partners from different Asian communities and different Asian countries are probably the most acceptable, though least common, unions to be found, while the most disadvantaged children are those who are the real victims of 'armies of occupation', for instance, the children of the many thousands of American servicemen who fathered youngsters in Vietnam, South Korea and the Philippines, most of whom grew up in a state of confusion and anxiety – many themselves turning to prostitution in adolescence – and few of whom ever joined their fathers in the United States, even if they knew their identity. In Vietnam, there have been several programmes designed to reunite American children with their natural fathers, but for those with the good or ill fortune to have long, straight noses and light brown hair the prospects of growing into adulthood in the US have been decreasing since the end of the war in Vietnam.

While the problems associated with the birth of Amerasian children continued in South Korea during 1993, some of the problems in the Philippines were reduced at the end of 1992 with the departure of the US military personnel. However, a new battle has been started – with a view to obtaining compensation from the US government. The battle may later continue in respect of children abandoned by Americans in

Vietnam and South Korea. In the *Philippine Daily Enquirer* on 28 February 1993, Shay Cullen, the head of the Preda Foundation in Olongapo city, wrote:

> Olongapo City has no relief programme or alternative employment programme for the thousands of women and children whose bodies once attracted tens of thousands of sailors and made politicians rich and powerful, autocratic and unmindful of their suffering ... The city's sex industry used women, and quickly threw them away to be replaced by young fresh bodies brought in from the provinces. Poverty was the best recruiter for the flesh market, hunger the lash from the master's whip ...
>
> One old grandmother wrote to me: 'I would like to ask for your help, especially in these hard times. I have no one to turn to for help. I am already 67 years old and my daughter left her five children with me. All are children of Americans who used to be boyfriends of my daughter while she was working in the bars. From the day they were born until now I have not received any support from their fathers or their mother. I alone have to provide for their needs from my income doing the laundry of others. I am old already and before I leave this world, I want them to be cared for. I want to entrust these children to you, Father. I know no one who can help but you. This is all I ask.'
>
> Thousands of bar women gave birth to children by US sailors. Many of these kids are now totally neglected and abandoned – a shameful legacy to a nation whose fine traditions and fundamental law give high priority to the welfare of women and children. But these traditions have been broken, and so has the Constitution by those sworn and paid to defend it. All these years, only charitable organisations have taken care of these throwaway children, even as politicians and club owners grew richer from the exploitation of the women. They are directly responsible and should be held accountable for the miseries these

women and children now suffer. They were the pimps, selling children as young as four years of age to Americans for sex, according to a US government undercover investigation conducted in Olongapo in 1988. The report was ignored by both Filipino and US authorities. But with the Clinton administration, things might change.

I was visiting a local school one day and there was a commotion. An Amerasian child, about 6, was throwing a tantrum in the school yard. She had been railed by her classmates with the chant: 'Your mother is a prostitute. You have no papa.'

Children can be cruel. But more so, adults. Last Wednesday, two children fled to the Preda Centre asking for help. They said they had been sexually abused for years by their stepfather. One was a five-year-old Amerasian.

Many adults lack understanding and compassion for the bar women. They say, 'They were prostitutes. They knew what they were doing, and now they should live with the consequences.'

I am not going to plead for compassion and justice for these children here. This should come naturally for those who have a conscience and a heart, and there are millions of Americans who have both and want to make things right for the throwaway children. US Embassy officials [in the Philippines] demonstrated such understanding when they approved the visas of four such children in three days without requiring their personal appearance. That is why the staff of the Preda Centre and I can leave for the US with the four children. Before the Federal Court in San Francisco, we will file a class action suit seeking justice for all Filipino-American children whoever they are.

We borrowed money for our fare and leave tomorrow.

The determination, dynamic approach and advocacy of Father Shay Cullen, the quality of self-sacrifice displayed by Liu Ip-wan, and the work undertaken by the Hong Kong Student

Aid Society (and other special centres in the region) are the approaches to child care in Asia that offer the best hope of bringing about changes in the gloomy picture already referred to. They and their successors provide the greatest hope for the generations to come.

The conclusion of this book must be that major shifts of attitude and policy are needed, with the intention of placing children at the forefront of local, national and regional concern. By the year 2010, as highlighted in the Preface, nearly 50 per cent of the population of Asian countries will be under 15 years of age. Most countries in the region have yet to take seriously their responsibility towards children and young people.

Children should command our attention and capture our imagination because of the potential power of the unique contribution of each individual born into this world. There is an early step to be taken. Each country should produce a policy paper on children, a document which flows from the principles of child care which it wishes to see upheld, preferably using the UN Convention on the Rights of the Child as a basis for its policy paper, and acknowledging to the maximum appropriate extent the culture and traditions of the country – provided that these do not run contrary to the fundamental rights of children in respect of their individual developmental needs. The principles of child care should, in this way, stem from the rights of all children to have their physical, social, emotional, psychological and environmental needs met.

Next, the range of interlocking health, educational and welfare services required to meet these needs must be identified. Here, every child with special needs – for instance, children at risk, children from low-income families, pre-delinquents, blind, deaf and handicapped children, children from broken homes and children in crisis – must be included.

New Civilisation

Principles of child care written into a policy document may require legislation, and will certainly demand increased levels of public and national commitment together with improvements in training for child care personnel in every area of concern. Child care will never be cheap. The question must be asked: Can we afford not to spend the maximum amount possible on children?

To conclude, I use the words of Alvin Toffler, who wrote in *The Third Wave*:

> A new civilization is emerging in our lives, and blind men everywhere are trying to supress it. The new civilization brings with it changed ways of working, loving and living; and beyond all this an altered consciousness as well . . . Most people . . . conceive of tomorrow as a mere extension of today, forgetting that trends no matter how seemingly powerful, do not merely continue in a linear fashion. They reach tipping points at which they explode into new phenomena.

The necessary degrees of change and progress are dependent upon this altered consciousness to which Toffler refers. To date, in respect of children without childhood in Southeast Asia, the signs are scarcely visible.

BIBLIOGRAPHY

An Analysis of the Situation of Children and Women in Indonesia, Jakarta, Indonesia, Central Bureau of Statistics, 1984

Asia 1991 Yearbook, Hong Kong, Far Eastern Economic Review 1992

Caplan, G., *An Approach to Community Mental Health*, London, Tavistock, 1969

Chamratrithirong, A., Yoddumnern-Attig, B., and Singhadej, O., *The Effect of Reduced Family Size on the Status of Maternal and Child Health*, Nakornpathom, Thailand, Mahidol University, 1984

Child Workers in Asia, Vol. 1, No. 2, October–December 1985; Vol. 2, No. 1, January–March 1986; Vol. 2, No. 3, July–September 1986; Vol. 3, No. 1, January–March 1987, Nos. 2 and 3, April–September 1987; No. 4, October–December 1987; Vol. 5, No. 1, January–March 1989, No. 2, April–June 1989, No. 3, July–September 1989

Danziger, R., *Health Action*, November 1990

Davis, L., *The Philippines: People, Poverty and Politics*, London, Macmillan, 1987

Davis, L., 'The Flipside of a Miracle', *Social Work Today*, 5 April 1990

Davis, L., 'Stolen Childhood', *World Mission*, Vol. 4, No. 11, December 1992

Delfs, R., privately circulated photocopy, source unknown

Emblen, V., and Vongsay, D., 'Pre-School Education in the

People's Republic of Laos', *Primary Teaching Studies*, Vol. 6, No. 2, October, London, Polytechnic of North London, 1991

Family Health International (article by Potts and Thapa), source unknown

Far Eastern Economic Review Asia and Pacific Atlas of Children in National Development, United Nations Children's Fund and United Nations Economic and Social Commission for Asia and the Pacific (ESCAP), UNICEF East Asia and Pakistan Regional Office, Bangkok, Thailand, 1988

Hamilton, D., *Sunday Express*, 8 November 1992

Kim, K.I., 'Child Abuse in Korea', paper presented at the VIII World Congress of Psychiatry, Athens, Greece, 12–19 October, 1988

Myers, R.G., *Toward a Fair Start for Children*, Paris, Unesco, 1991. *Situation Analysis of Children and Women in Indonesia*, Jakarta, Government of Indonesia – UNICEF, December 1988, revised April 1989

Pringle, M.L.K., *The Needs of Children*, London, Hutchinson, 1974

Piet, D., and Piet, N., *Family Planning and the Banjars of Bali* (source unknown), 1982

Toffler, A., *The Third Wave*, New York, Morrow, 1980

Vittachi, A., Stolen Childhood, Oxford, Polity, 1989